About Access Archaeology

Access Archaeology offers a different publishing model for specialist academic material that might traditionally prove commercially unviable, perhaps due to its sheer extent or volume of colour content, or simply due to its relatively niche field of interest.

All *Access Archaeology* publications are available in open-access e-pdf format and in (on-demand) print format. The open-access model supports dissemination in areas of the world where budgets are more severely limited, and also allows individual academics from all over the world the chance to access the material privately, rather than relying solely on their university or public library. Print copies, nevertheless, remain available to individuals and institutions who need or prefer them.

The material is professionally refereed, but not peer reviewed. Copy-editing takes place prior to submission of the work for publication and is the responsibility of the author. Academics who are able to supply print-ready material are not charged any fee to publish (including making the material available in open-access). In some instances the material is type-set in-house and in these cases a small charge is passed on for layout work.

This model works for us as a publisher because we are able to publish specialist work with relatively little editorial investment. Our core effort goes into promoting the material, both in open-access and print, where *Access Archaeology* books get the same level of attention as our core peer-reviewed imprint by being included in marketing e-alerts, print catalogues, displays at academic conferences and more, supported by professional distribution worldwide.

Open-access allows for greater dissemination of the academic work than traditional print models, even lithographic printing, could ever hope to support. It is common for a new open-access e-pdf to be downloaded several hundred times in its first month since appearing on our website. Print sales of such specialist material would take years to match this figure, if indeed it ever would.

By printing 'on-demand', meanwhile, (or, as is generally the case, maintaining minimum stock quantities as small as two), we are able to ensure orders for print copies can be fulfilled without having to invest in great quantities of stock in advance. The quality of such printing has moved forward radically, even in the last few years, vastly increasing the fidelity of images (highly important in archaeology) and making colour printing more economical.

Access Archaeology is a vehicle that allows us to publish useful research, be it a PhD thesis, a catalogue of archaeological material or data, in a model that does not cost more than the income it generates.

This model may well evolve over time, but its ambition will always remain to publish archaeological material that would prove commercially unviable in traditional publishing models, without passing the expense on to the academic (author or reader).

EGYPTIAN PREDYNASTIC ANTHROPOMORPHIC OBJECTS

A study of their function and significance in Predynastic burial customs

Ryna Ordynat

Access Archaeology

ARCHAEOPRESS PUBLISHING LTD
Gordon House
276 Banbury Road
Oxford OX2 7ED

www.archaeopress.com

ISBN 978 1 78491 778 4
ISBN 978 1 78491 779 1 (e-Pdf)

© Archaeopress and R Ordynat 2018

Cover: Female Figure, ca. 3500-3400 B.C.E. Terracotta, pigment, 11 1/2 x 5 1/2 x 2 1/4 in. (29.2 x 14 x 5.7 cm). Brooklyn Museum, Charles Edwin Wilbour Fund, 07.447.505. Creative Commons-BY (Photo: Brooklyn Museum, 07.447.505_SL1.jpg)

Printed and bound in Great Britain by
Marston Book Services Ltd, Oxfordshire

All rights reserved. No part of this book may be reproduced or transmitted,
in any form or by any means, electronic, mechanical, photocopying or otherwise,
without the prior written permission of the copyright owners.

CONTENTS

ACKNOWLEDGEMENTS iii

CHAPTER 1: INTRODUCTION 1
1.1 BACKGROUND AND THE DATA 1
1.2 MAIN RESEARCH QUESTION 3
1.3 THE ISSUE OF STATUS... 3
1.4 METHODOLOGICAL APPROACH 5

CHAPTER 2: THE STUDY OF PREDYNATIC FIGURINES 7
2.1 EARLY EXCAVATION REPORTS... 7
2.2 PETER UCKO AND THE BEGINNING OF FIGURINE STUDIES 8
2.3 ANTHROPOMOPHIC OBJECTS IN THE PREDYNASTIC 9
2.4 THE STUDY OF PREDYNASTIC ICONOGRAPHY 11
2.5 PREDYNASTIC MORTUARY STUDIES 12
2.6 THE SOCIAL PERSPECTIVE... 13

CHAPTER 3: METHODS OF ANALYSIS 17
3.1 INTRODUCTION... 17
    3.1.1 PHYSICAL PROPERTIES... 17
    3.1.2 DECORATION AND DESIGN... 18
    3.1.3 VALUE 19
    3.1.4 IDENTITY 19
3.2 MATERIAL ENGAGEMENT AND PERSONHOOD 19
3.3 OBJECTS AND MORTUARY ARCHAEOLOGY THEORY 21
3.4 SEX, IDENTITY AND MATERIAL CULTURE 21
3.5 THE CATALOGUE 22
    3.5.1 TYPE OF OBJECT 22
    3.5.2 DATE 22
    3.5.3 LOCATION 22
    3.5.4 GRAVE NUMBER 23
    3.5.5 MATERIAL... 23
    3.5.6 SEX OF OBJECT 23
    3.5.7 CONDITION OF OBJECT 23
    3.5.8 POSITION OF OBJECT IN THE GRAVE.. 23
    3.5.9 SEX OF ASSOCIATED BODY OR BODIES 23
    3.5.10 GRAVE CONDITION 24
    3.5.11 ASSOCIATED OBJECTS AND MATERIALS... 24
3.6 DETERMINING THE SEX OF TUSKS, TAGS AND COMBS 24
3.7 DATA ANALYSIS 25
3.8 PROBLEMS AND DIFFICULTIES 26

CHAPTER 4: ANALYSIS AND RESULTS 29
4.1 SUMMARY OF THE DATA 29
4.2 DETERMINING SEX OF ANTHROPOMORPHIC OBJECTS 30
4.3 PLACEMENT OF OBJECTS 30
4.4 OBJECT GROUPINGS 33
4.5 OBJECT ASSOCIATIONS 34
4.6 RELATIONSHIP BETWEEN SEX OF THE BODY AND SEX OF THE OBJECT 35
4.7 OBJECT MATERIALS 35
4.8 OBJECT BREAKAGE PATTERNS 37
4.9 SIMILAR OBJECTS IN DIFFERENT GRAVES 37

CHAPTER 5: DISCUSSION 39
5.1 INTRODUCTION 39
5.2 PLACEMENT OF OBJECTS 41
5.3 OBJECT GROUPINGS 45
5.4 OBJECT ASSOCIATIONS 46
5.5 SIMILAR OBJECTS IN DIFFERENT GRAVES 48
5.6 RELATIONSHIP BETWEEN SEX OF THE BODY AND SEX OF THE OBJECT 48
5.7 MATERIALS 51
5.8 OBJECT BREAKAGE 53
5.9 THEORIES ON FUNCTION 55

CHAPTER 6: CONCLUSION 57

APPENDIX I: THE OBJECT CATALOGUE 61

APPENDIX II: ADDITIONAL GRAVES 71
MATMAR 71
MAHASNA 71
NAQADA 71
MOSTAGEDDA 71

APPENDIX III: ASSOCIATED OBJECTS 73

APPENDIX IV - LIST OF OBJECTS AND FIGURES 77

FIGURES 91

BIBLIOGRAPHY 111

ACKNOWLEDGEMENTS

It is a pleasure to thank the many people who made this work possible.

Firstly, I would like to thank my supervisor, Dr. Ashten Warfe. With his help, inspiration, and unwavering interest in my work, he helped me stay motivated and enthusiastic, and get through the more difficult times. He provided encouragement, sound advice, good teaching and guidance, and a multitude of good ideas, and I am sincerely grateful to him for all his help.

I would also like to thank my secondary supervisor, Dr. Colin Hope, for sharing his wisdom and knowledge with me, and providing helpful insight and information. I am also grateful to the staff and fellow students at the Centre of Ancient Cultures at Monash University, for their advice and support.

Lastly, I would like to thank my family and friends for all their love and encouragement, and for their constant support and faith in me. Also, I would like to say a big thank you to Kristine for reading through my work and providing so many useful suggestions. And most of all I would like to thank my loving, supportive, encouraging, and patient partner Oliver, without whose faithful support during the most difficult stages, this work would never have been completed. Thank you.

CHAPTER 1: INTRODUCTION

1.1 BACKGROUND AND THE DATA

Representing the human image is one of the earliest compulsions of the human mind. The first attempts at art were made by humans more than 30,000 years ago, being one of the earliest indications of human cognition of both symbolic and abstract understanding (Conkey 1987, Halverston 1992, Morriss-Kay 2010). The famous 'Venus' figurines are some of the first and most commonly known human portable depictions, appearing in Upper Palaeolithic sites throughout Eurasia, and are thought to be strongly exaggerated representations of female fertility (Morris Kay 2010, 166). Such representations, in the form of a figurine are in themselves an attempt to depict some form of reality or to make a statement, contests the renowned figurine scholar Douglas Bailey (2013, 245). It is also commonly accepted that the motivation behind the making of such objects was for a particular function, which is usually thought to be empowering fertility (Rice 1981, 402). Interpretations such as these have remained very common for prehistoric female figurines, yet in recent years there has been an increase of interest and research in the topic, producing several new studies and many alternative theories and views (McDermott 1996, Volkova 2012).

In his study on prehistoric female figurines from various places, Lesure (2002, 587) notes that small figurines are a common find at archaeological sites of early villages - the figurines are predominantly of humans, and appear to be functioning primarily as household objects. Lesure (2002, 2011) also brings into prominence the relevance of female imagery in particular. The pattern is not entirely exclusive, but the frequency of it has led to it being linked with fertility cults or goddess interpretations, and evolved into a general assumption that figurines are usually part of a natural, primal religion common to all early cultures, such as a mother goddess cult (Lesure 2002, 587). These perpetuations of Western assumptions about symbolism of gender and fertility have recently been intensely criticised, especially from the feminist perspective (Lesure 2011, Talalay 1993, Meskell 1995). The current understanding of human figurines has now been extended well beyond the limitations of a mother-goddess interpretation, encompassing much deeper and more subtle details of the human psyche, and what it means to be both human and an individual (Bailey 2013, 261).

The Predynastic period was an extension of the Egyptian Neolithic, stretching approximately between 4500 BCE and 3000 BCE, with major settlements focused in Upper Egypt between Qena and Luxor, and Lower Egypt in the Nile Delta (Midant-Reyenes 2000, 169). Major cultural developments in Upper Egypt, which are the main focal point of this stdy, were located around the excavated settlements at El-Badari, Naqada, Abydos and Hierakonpolis, among many others, and Maadi and Buto in Lower Egypt. The earliest Badarian settlement sites at Hemamieh, first excavated by Gertrude Caton-Thompson and Guy Brunton, would have had an average of 50 to 200 people, occupying small hearth based dwellings (Midant-Reyenes 2000, 183). Larger, rectangular and more numerous and dense structures were found at the Hierakonpolis settlement, indicating an emergence of a more sophisticated Naqada I culture (Midant-Reyenes 2000, 185). The social organisation of these early societies was dominated by a dynamic iconography, with the addition of military, economic and political power developing probably due to increasing competition, both military and economic, between these different states (Andelkovic 2011, 27). This development of the imagery and iconography of political power is evident in many decorative elements of the material culture, including mace heads, knife handles, pottery, palettes and rock art (Andelkovic 2011, 28).

Human depiction is by no means unusual in the Egyptian Predynastic period, from approximately 4500 BCE to 3300 BCE (Hendrickx 2006). Art and iconography in this period play a significant role in the lead up to the formation state control in Egypt, and the institutionalising of iconography during the early Dynastic period. Predynastic depictions of the human form are incredibly diverse – they extend over many forms, including decorated pottery, rock art, tomb painting, painted linen and palettes from the period (Capart 1905, Petrie 1920, Scamuzzi 1965, Midant-Reyenes 2000, Garfinkel 2003, Eyckerman and Hendrickx 2012). A variety of three-dimensional objects shaped the in human image form a subset of this collection of Predynastic artefacts. These include human figurines, hippopotamus tusks carved with human heads and features, tag pendants and hair combs in human shape, and vessels shaped into a human form or with sculpted human figures prominently attached to their rims. The variety of these objects has drawn the attention of Egyptologists since their first discovery, and they have since been examined in several prominent studies (Capart 1905, Petrie 1920, Baumgartel 1960, Ucko 1968, Hassan 1992, Eyckerman and Hendrickx 2011a). The materials from which these objects are made are diverse, ranging from clay to vegetable paste, ivory, and varieties of stone and other materials. Both males and females are represented, sometimes in elaborate detail and at other times abstractly and schematically.

These objects are extremely rare, appearing in less than 1% of the many thousands of burials excavated from the Predynastic period. A problem for the Predynastic studies is the fact that almost everything we know and understand about the culture of the period stems from the archaeological evidence found at the numerous cemeteries, excavated mainly in the early 20th century. Indeed, cemeteries and the bodies and objects that have been recovered there form the largest portion of evidence on which the study of Predynastic Egypt is based. The burials themselves are often disturbed or plundered, leaving us with no information about the sex of the occupant, the types of goods that were interred with them, and the original placement of these goods in the grave. However, a sufficient number of graves have remained intact to warrant a study of the possible patterns in which anthropomorphic objects were deposited. The particular focus of this study will be on the specific placements of the anthropomorphic objects themselves and their possible associations with other grave goods in order to ascertain if there are any patterns. The study will also focus on the sex of the bodies in relationship to the objects and the materials used to make the objects.

The focus of previous studies of the three-dimensional human image has most frequently been on iconography, examining the typology and the appearance of the objects in order to determine their possible function in the ritual and symbolic spheres (Baumgartel 1960, Ucko 1968). Little attention has been paid to the specific placement of such objects in the grave, and the relationships and significance indicated by such particular placements. Predynastic cemeteries are formidable repositories of material culture, with graves positively stacked with material things, surrounding the buried individual. Human three-dimensional depictions formed part of such assemblages, and yet it is not fully understood why. Were they representations of individuals, ancestor figures or deities? Did they have a specific role to play in the burial itself, perhaps of a protective nature? Were they functional every-day objects of value to the buried individual that were taken by them into the graves, perhaps to be used again in the next life? In addition to answering these questions, an attempt to understand the emotions and aesthetic considerations that may have played a part in determining the placement of anthropomorphic objects in the grave will be made in the course of this study. Such concepts have been previously introduced to the study of Predynastic burials by Stevenson (2007a, 2009a), and they will form a large part of the study's methodological framework. Finally, as the reason of why such objects were placed in Predynastic graves has not yet been fully ascertained, it will be the overarching aim of this work to offer further possible speculations and insights on this issue. The study will attempt to broaden the topic by introducing alternative views of the anthropomorphic objects' interpretations, such as the theories of material culture and mortuary analysis, as well as ethnography.

1.2 MAIN RESEARCH QUESTION

The focus of this work is the study of Egyptian anthropomorphic objects dating from approximately 3700 BCE to 3300 BCE, which comprises late Naqada I to Naqada II cultural periods in Predynastic Egypt. The body of data analysed will include a specific set of objects related to the human form: figurines, tusks, tags, combs, vessels and fragments.

The aim of the analysis will be to identify patterns of placement, and connections between the sex of the body and the object. The study will analyse all Predynastic anthropomorphic objects that have been found in graves in their original burial context. The aim of such an analysis will be to understand the meaning and significance of the objects in the burials they were placed in, especially in regards to their possible association or relationship to the deceased.

The work will ask why anthropomorphic three-dimensional objects were placed in Predynastic graves and formed part of the grave assemblage, and what does their placement tell us about Predynastic burial customs. The aim is to provide patterns for which there are good grounds, and then to speculate on the results, rather than to determine the exact meaning or function of the objects themselves. Answering this question of placement will require considering whether the anthropomorphic element held particular significance or value in Predynastic culture, and whether the objects themselves were of essentially ritual, social or practical nature in their burial context. The initial response that can be formulated at the commencement of this study, based on previous suggestions and interpretations from Predynastic research, such as Ucko (1968) and Stevenson (2013), is that these objects held a particular value in a social, personal and ritual way. A further discussion of the literature that has been produced on this topic, as well as on mortuary theory, has been included in Chapter 2. Chapter 3 will then present the methodological approach of the project, dwelling in detail on the mortuary and material culture theories and ideas that will be used to interpret the data, as well as on the construction of the database itself, and on the ways the objects have been sorted and catalogued. In the course of the analysis in Chapter 4, the hypothesis of the placement of objects signifying importance and function will be tested though a search for patterns in the placement of these objects in the grave, as well as any evident connections made with the contents of the grave itself (such as any particular association with another object, or between the sex of the object and the grave occupant). Finally, in Chapter 5, this hypothesis will be tested and discussed, together with the results accumulated in the process of the analysis, in an attempt to produce reasons for the objects' presence in Predynastic graves.

1.3 THE ISSUE OF STATUS

This is a specific question related to the main research question that will be touched on briefly. It is the frequently discussed question of whether anthropomorphic objects, and figurines especially, are predominantly found in more elaborate and 'wealthy' burials (Bard 1994). Such an enquiry is complicated for several reasons: firstly, the number of surviving intact graves is very small, which necessarily complicates attempts at speculation on this issue. However, this point is frequently touched upon in the studies of figurines and other anthropomorphic objects from the Predynastic. For example, Ucko (1968, 181) states, in his well-known work on Predynastic figurines:

> 'It is necessary to consider Baumgartel's (1951, pp. 56-8) contention that figurines are found in tombs of exceptionally rich and important people. This contention cannot be accepted. It is not assuming too much to presume that had the tomb been especially rich in tomb goods the excavator concerned would have published some account of them. The tombs mentioned above which contained figurines, but whose funerary goods have never received adequate

publication shows that splendour of grave goods and the presence of figurines do not necessarily go together... Figurines, therefore, were occasionally placed in tombs where they belonged to the rich or the poor.'

Likewise, Midant-Reynes (2000, 175) states:

'The analysis of the other grave goods shows that the burials containing figurines were not particularly 'rich' in other respects, and in fact such sculpted figures might sometimes be the only funerary offering in the tomb.'

This assumption that anthropomorphic objects are predominantly found in more elaborate, wealthy graves has been perpetuated in the discussion of Predynastic figurines since the reports of their discovery began to be published in the early 20th century. Yet this assumption has not been supported by any conclusive evidence, since a thorough analysis of the figurines' context has not been attempted until now. One of the analytical enquiries of this project will be to conduct such a data analysis, and to form a conclusion about whether these objects are predominantly found in 'wealthier' graves with luxury items, or whether there is, in fact, no clear correlation with the wealth of the burial. A discussion of whether such an analysis is necessary when interpreting this group of objects as a whole will be entered into in the subsequent chapters.

Predynastic figurines are usually treated as a separate group of objects from tusks, tags or combs; however it was decided that for the purposes of this study the other three-dimensional anthropomorphic data will also be included and examined. This is due to the database of provenanced figurines being too small for an extensive analysis, and therefore tusks, tags and other anthropomorphic objects will form a useful point of comparison in conducting the analysis of their function. The data used will be presented in a catalogue including every grave that contained anthropomorphic objects dating between the late Naqada I and Naqada II, with a total of 59 graves analysed. The time parameters that have been chosen are a means of limiting the date of the objects within a relatively restricted time period, rather than allowing for over a thousand years of artistic, cultural, iconographical and symbolic development of the whole Predynastic period to serve as an impediment for as unbiased an analysis as possible. The graves are organised according to the cemetery locations – these include, in catalogue order, El-Badari, Qau, Mostagedda, El-Mahasna, El-Amrah, Abadiya, Ballas, Naqada, El-Ma'mariya, Abydos and Hierakonpolis (for Map, see Figure 1). The catalogue consists of categories that include: tomb number, date, number of objects, sex of object, condition of object (broken or whole), object material (clay, ivory, etc), object's position in the grave, tomb condition (Plundered/Disturbed/Intact) and sex of the body.

A total of 118 anthropomorphic objects have been recorded in this analysis. The objects included in this database came only from graves, and as the aims of the work do not include a typological analysis, or an analysis of the object's appearance and design, it will not include any purchased or unprovenanced objects. The objects are found in graves of men, women and children, buried with a diverse range of grave goods, the numbers of which range from only a few to a vast quantity. The number and type of objects also varies from grave to grave and from a single up to 16 objects in one grave.

All the figurines and some tags were sexed based on the appearance of genitalia (breasts, pubic triangle, or penis sheath), or in their absence, on waist to hip ratio (Nowak 2004, Brovarski 2005, Patch 2011). It appears to be a standard feature for most Predynastic female figurines to have a narrow waist and full hips. A further detailed discussion on the determination of the sex of the object forms part of the studies' methodology and can be found in Chapter 3.

1.4 METHODOLOGICAL APPROACH

Smaller lines of enquiry will form part of the larger over-arching research question of this study. These will examine whether the objects are predominantly found in graves of men, women, or children whether the sex of the object (if possible to determine) and the sex of the deceased individual deposited in the burial correspond, and if there are any repeating patterns in the manner in which the figurines were deposited in the grave (i.e. their position relative to the body and other grave goods, and their condition).

The final discussion will focus on how much it is possible to speculate, using the results of the grave analysis, on the nature of the function of anthropomorphic objects. Discussion points will include ascertaining whether the objects may have been ritual items or highly personal items related to the individual buried in the grave, and whether more evidence may be required to reach a substantial conclusion about their function. These objects undoubtedly played an important role in burial practices and customs of Predynastic Egyptians, as they are usually given a prominent place in the burial itself. For example, the 4 ivory figurines from the intact grave 271 at Naqada were inserted into an area of clean sand in the grave, parallel to the body (Petrie 1895, 32), (Figure 97). This ostentatious positioning of human figurines is unique and most prominent in the grave, and seems to indicate their special importance in this particular burial. Human figures and depictions, however, occur extremely rarely in graves in general. They do not appear in every Predynastic cemetery; therefore it could be assumed that the practice of burying human images with the dead varied locally. In addition, many graves have been plundered and disturbed, leaving their original contents and positions of the goods in the grave unknown. It is hard to overcome such a gap in information, and undoubtedly it poses a significant problem to this study. However, the intention here is to form an analysis based on what is available to us today, in order to construct a sound interpretation of this material and its burial context. The resulting conclusions may point to the contrary, and there is a possibility that there will not be enough prominent patterns in the objects deposition and placement, or simply not enough intact evidence. Whatever the outcome of this study is, it will nonetheless make an attempt to bring all the available evidence together from various sources in order to determine exactly how much the context can tell us about the function of anthropomorphic imagery in the Predynastic mortuary realm.

CHAPTER 2: THE STUDY OF PREDYNATIC FIGURINES

2.1 EARLY EXCAVATION REPORTS

The early excavation reports form an essential part of the literature that will be used in this study, as these provide details of the first time Predynastic anthropomorphic objects were uncovered. Additionally, some of the reports put forward theories on the function of these objects. The reports that did include the 1902 report 'El-Amrah and Abydos, 1899-1901' by Randall-MacIver and Mace, the 1911 report 'Pre-Dynastic Cemetery at El-Mahasna' by Ayrton and Loat, and 'Prehistoric Egypt' by Petrie, published in 1920.

In their 1902 report on El-Amrah and Abydos, Randall-MacIver and Mace briefly discuss both the figurines and the tusks and tags they found in the graves, concluding about the former that they are 'portraits of natives and not foreigners' (Randall-MacIver and Mace 1902, 42). About the latter they state that they may have formed part of a sorcerer's outfit, or they may have been used in dance rituals, similar to the ivory wands that were used for the same purpose in the historical periods (Randall-MacIver and Mace 1902, 48). Ayrton and Loat (1911, 26), in a section of their report on El-Mahasna cemetery, discuss tusks as possible magical objects, comparing them to 'similar horns...used on the west coast of Africa to catch and imprison a man's spirit'. Petrie first discovered female figurines during his excavations at Ballas and Naqada (1896) and at Abadiya and Diospolis Parva (1901), and maintained an interest in them throughout his later excavations. He published a study of Predynastic bought figurines from his collection at University College London, making detailed comments on their style and development (Petrie 1920, 6-10), but focusing his interpretation primarily on tusks and tags. He suggests several uses for these objects, including tusks as hunting trophies, or tags used for plugging up water-skins (Petrie 1920, 34). His concluding statement on their function is particularly significant for this work: 'We need the clearance of a well-preserved and intact grave to settle the question' (Petrie 1920, 34).

Other important early publications of excavation reports mentioning anthropomorphic objects, on which much of the later and current studies are based, are those of Guy Brunton's excavation at Mostagedda (1937) and Matmar (1948) and Brunton and Caton-Thompson's work at El-Badari (1928). Brunton and Caton Thompson published extensive and detailed descriptions of where most of the Badarian figurines were found – these included the three most prominent examples, not included in this study due to the early period they date to. The figurines varied greatly in size, style and material – one was made from ivory and incised in detail, another from fired clay, and another from unfired clay. Brunton and Caton-Thompson offered no suggestions on function, referring to Petrie's above-mentioned theories in his 1920 publication. Other early excavation reports in which figurines are mentioned include Henri De Morgan's (1912) published report on the excavations at El-Ma'mariya. The most recent findings include Friedman's work at Hierakonpolis (2003), which has recently unearthed several new anthropomorphic objects in Predynastic tombs, and Dreyer's recent excavations at Abydos (Dreyer et. al. 1998), which discussed the grave in which the famous figurine vessel (Figure 70) was discovered.

Early excavation reports, though very useful in providing information concerning the origin of the objects analysed in this project, lack the consistency and reliability of modern archaeological reports. However, it is important to remember that such reports defined the standards used by archaeologists today, even if they did not approach the same level of meticulous attention to detail in both excavation techniques and the recording of data. Yet it does make it difficult to utilise this material when, for example, the age and sex of the bodies are frequently not recorded. Additionally, graves or objects which were thought to be of lesser significance (some of which unfortunately included anthropomorphic objects) were either poorly described or not mentioned at all. The preoccupation with race and racial depiction also frequently influenced the descriptions of figurines provided by the excavator. All these factors make it difficult to extract the necessary information for such an analysis, and it is clear that the descriptions and interpretations of anthropomorphic objects given by the excavators need to be viewed with caution.

In addition to these reports, museum catalogues by Needler (1984) for the Brooklyn Museum in New York, by Payne (1993) for the Ashmolean Museum in Oxford, and more recently by Patch (2011) for a Predynastic art exhibition for the Metropolitan Museum of Art, were of primary assistance when constructing a database of figurines and related objects. These catalogues usually offer a basic estimated date for the objects, and a summary of theories regarding the objects' function derived from earlier statements from Petrie or Ucko, whose work will be discussed in detail later in this chapter.

2.2 PETER UCKO AND THE BEGINNING OF FIGURINE STUDIES

The most important and influential study on Predynastic anthropomorphic objects is Ucko's 1968 catalogue, *Anthropomorphic Figurines of Predynastic Egypt and Neolithic Crete, with Comparative Material from the Prehistoric Near East and Mainland Greece.* This key work forms a basis and a reference for all later figurine studies, since no equivalent study has been attempted to date. Ucko's catalogue, though an unparalleled achievement in documenting and understanding Predynastic figurines, has its limitations. An analysis of figurines from all periods of the Predynastic, encompassing over a 1,000 years of development and change, and the inclusion purchased and unprovenanced figurines into the analysis further complicates Ucko's conclusions about the functions of these objects. In terms of interpretation, Ucko begins with a critique of the earliest assumptions about female figurines from ancient cultures, including Egyptian figurines. The assumptions were based on the supposed wide-spread Mother Goddess cult, first suggested and advocated by Marija Gimbutas (Murray 1956, 89; Ucko 1968, 415; Gimbutas 1999), This theory has now been reviewed and largely dismissed by most scholars (Meskell 1995; 1998, Talalay 1994, Graves-Brown 2010, Bailey 1994). In conjunction with this theory, female figurines have been suggested to represent Predynastic deities or Early Dynastic goddesses by some scholars (David 2002, 52). The Mother Goddess theory is usually applied to European and Near Eastern cultures; however, it has influenced the interpretation of Predynastic Egyptian female figurines, which Ucko acknowledges and criticises (Ucko 1968, 413). Ucko then continues his discussion of the figurines' function by steering it to new possibilities not suggested before. He states that his aim is to find 'as many practices as possible which could explain the making of small figurines' (Ucko 1968, 420), which if not entirely practical, at least serves the purpose of broadening the interpretation possibilities from that of fertility idols, a hitherto designated and standard interpretation of prehistoric figurines. Ucko proposed several new ideas about figurine functions and had a profound influence on later scholarship in this area. Drawing on many other studies of figurines from various ancient cultures, as well as on ethnographic evidence, he suggests new and innovative ways of analysing and studying figurines. He stresses the importance of the burial context, arguing that the figurines ought to be treated first and foremost as burial objects in any attempted interpretation (Ucko 1962; 1969). His suggestions of what the figurines might have represented include mourners, servant or initiation figures, on account of them being found close to the body, therefore directly used in mortuary ritual (Ucko 1968, 429-432). He also suggests they may be vehicles of sympathetic magic, used in medicinal or magical rituals in daily life (Ucko 1968, 431). Ucko (1968, 432-434) speculates on the possibility that they may simply be dolls, made to be children's toys and serving a much simpler function in everyday life. The strongest concluding message of Ucko's study is of diversity, emphasising that such figurines may have had multiple functions both in everyday life and in death (Ucko 1968, 426).

Ucko refers frequently to the work of Elise Baumgartel, another pioneer in systematic and comprehensive study of Predynastic anthropomorphic objects. Unlike Ucko, Baumgartel's work encompasses decorated tusks and tags for the first time since Petrie's earlier mention of them in 1920. Baumgartel (1960, 71) focused on the funerary ritual aspect associated with these objects, and especially with the female figurines. She argues that they may have had some motherhood symbolism, drawing attention to early Old Kingdom depictions of mother and child in graves as a supplication for children (Baumgartel 1960, 71). She also draws attention to the fact that it is unwise to examine female figurines in isolation, suggesting that male and animal figurines have also been frequently found in graves and may have been similarly ritually significant (Baumgartel 1960, 71-72). When discussing tusks and tags, Baumgartel (1955, 60) points out for the first time the size and mobility of such small objects, suggesting they were used 'for manipulation in the hand' and therefore must have had different associations and meanings to those of human figurines. Although neither Baumgartel's nor Ucko's studies of figurines are entirely complete, and do not include a thoroughly documented analysis of the funerary context of anthropomorphic objects, they are works of primary importance to such an analysis as is attempted in this project.

2.3 ANTHROPOMOPHIC OBJECTS IN THE PREDYNASTIC

Anthropomorphic objects, and in particular figurines, usually appear in the studies of Predynastic Egypt selectively, and as part of a discussion about Predynastic art, iconography, mortuary practices or religion (Capart 1905, Hornblower 1929, Kantor 1944, Murray 1956, Garfinkel 2003, Wilkinson 2003, Midant-Reynes 2000, Wengrow 2006). The only comprehensive and well-known study, with the exception of Capart's (1905) earlier general work on Predynastic art and objects and Petrie's (1920) volume on the same subject was completed by Ucko in 1968. Several theses have also been written on the subject by students of art history and theology (Spradling Hoglund 1983, Relke 2001). As for the interpretations of the figurines themselves, those that have been most accepted are generally only related to their iconographic significance. Due to the fact that most figurines have been found in graves it is sometimes assumed that they were part of a wide spread mortuary cult practice across Upper Egypt in many of the major excavated cemeteries. Some scholars build on this idea to say that the figurines' functions can be narrowed down to use only in a funerary cult, since they were almost never found in settlement context, and therefore they could not be dolls, votive objects or ancestor representations, or used for any domestic or practical purposes (Baumgartel 1960; 1970). Other suggestions for their purposes in the grave include a donor, praying for children, or a representation of a specific deity, whose image protects the dead and helps them in the afterlife (Lesko 1999, 10). They have also been considered to be representations of the early versions of Dynastic deities (Hassan 1998), or as early servant representations, based on the dynastic idea of shabti statues (Patch 2011, 115). Figurines in graves are also proposed as embodying a particular aspect of the deceased, either social or physical (Midant-Reyens 1992, 175). There are several examples that support this theory, including the figurines that were found on the body, or imitating its position closely (Eyckerman and Hendrickx 2011b, 425; Harrington 2004, 35). Small figurines with overt sexual characteristics have also been regarded as symbolising the deceased's sexuality or rebirth (Harrington 2004, 36). Unfortunately, a common feature of such interpretations in general Predynastic studies is the detachment of the author from the objects' original context. The theories of function, first suggested by Petrie, and later asserted by Ucko, are sometimes being repeated without further inquiry into the original state and context.

Due to the lack of intact data, the database composed for this research combines all three-dimensional anthropomorphic objects dating approximately to the Naqada II period. Contrary to this decision, there has long existed a divide between figurines and the decorated ivory objects (tusks, tags and combs) in Predynastic iconography and funerary studies. So far, only the works that touch on Predynastic figurines have been discussed, and these are much more numerous than the studies of tusks, tags and combs. The most significant studies to deal specifically with this category of objects include those by Nowak (2004), Brovarski (2005) and Eyckerman and Hendrickx (2011a). As Hendrickx's work is discussed in more detail in a separate section below, here the focus will be on Nowak's and Brovarski's contribution. Nowak (2004, 900) highlights important details in the appearance of anthropomorphic ivory objects, identifying their image, size and material as being extremely similar, and contrasting them to figurines, which are characterised by their diversity and variety. Additionally, she highlights an important factor of the disappearance of these objects and motifs in the early Dynastic period, making it clear that theories of function cannot safely be based on any later Dynastic examples (Nowak 2004, 903). In terms of interpretation, Nowak dismisses Petrie's earlier theory of tusks being hunting trophies exclusively used by men, and points out that tusks are frequently associated with female burials. Nowak (2004, 869) suggests that if the tusks were indeed associated with hunting, women must have actively participated in such activities. When discussing tags, Nowak (2004, 899) examines their context closely, and supports Petrie's initial idea of tags being magical objects, forming part of a sorcerer's or fortune teller's outfit, but ultimately admitting that due to the present state of data it is not really possible to determine a specific function, only adding that there must have been one. Brovarski (2005, 226) pays special attention to combs, classing them among other ivory objects as 'objects of daily use, specifically objects de toilette', but with possible magical or protective significance embedded in them. Brovarski (2005, 226) emphasises the significance and individuality of the carved image, its protective powers and personal significance to the owner. A final point Brovarski (2005, 227) makes is that such objects must have been produced by a group of independent craftsmen supported by the larger community, a factor that is evident in the mastery these artists had over the materials they worked.

In addition to the studies that have been done specifically on Predynastic anthropomorphic objects, it is useful to review the studies on figurines from other prehistoric cultures. This cross-cultural comparison method has some merit as it provides alternative models and theories on figurine studies, as in some cases the methodologies and frameworks that have been used in these studies can be applied to the Predynastic figurines. Notable examples of such works include Bailey (1994, 2005, 2013), Hamilton (1996) and Lesure (2002, 2011). Lesure (2002, 593), in constructing methodologies for interpreting figurines, selects four different cultures (Near East, Mesoamerica, Southwest America and Japan), and concludes that different figurine studies face similar challenges, problems and restrictions in interpretation, even though their objects of study had different meanings. He draws attention to the complexity and accessibility of the figurines' meaning to the makers and actors involved and to such meanings being internal or socially external (Lesure 2002, 594). Lesure (2002, 593) also suggests that the meaning of a figurine could be beyond what the figurine physically portrays, referencing abstract concepts or ideas intuitively known and understood by the makers and contemporaries of that culture. These concepts, Lesure (2002, 594) argues, can be defined through available sources of evidence, including indigenous and ethnographic commentary, archaeological context and analogies. Lesure's framework for a successful and productive figurine analysis is to employ several methods and sources of information (human universal, early and prehistoric general information, and theory of the structure of social formation, analogies and ethnographies), while acknowledging the largest problem with using analogy as a method is its inability to deal with variability, especially regional variability.

Bailey's methodology (2007) is similar in its approach to Lesure's. He attempts to study the context, iconography and imagery of prehistoric figurines that emerged at similar times around the world through a universalist approach, testing the relationships of figurines and early pottery and their possible connection to fertility (Bailey 2007, 32-33). This approach does produce some interesting results, as Bailey concludes that the connection with early pottery and fertility cannot be used as a universal explanation for the meaning of female figurines (2007, 39). In his analysis of figurines from Neolithic Europe, he attempts to view the figurines as representations of individuals (1994, 323). Similarly to Ucko, he stresses that the accuracy depends not only on the visual examination of the figurine, but on the identification of the represented subject, and a detailed knowledge of the archaeological and social context of both figurine and subject represented (1994, 329). Bailey (2013, 260) further suggests that elements of the body and decoration in the figurine may be less significant than the personification and abstract understanding of the body, constructing society's definitions of identity, gender and the body.

2.4 THE STUDY OF PREDYNASTIC ICONOGRAPHY

In recent years, some figurines have been brought to more prominence by the studies of Hendrickx (2002; 2009; 2011a; 2011b; 2012) and Hassan (1998, 2002, and 2004). Focusing more on the iconographic aspects for their interpretations, they propose a theory which suggests that the figurines are connected to a bovine fertility cult possibly practiced in Predynastic Egypt. This theory is based on Predynastic art imagery, including pottery decoration, rock art and a collection of the only excavated female figurines with upraised arms from two graves at the cemetery at El-Ma'mariya. Hassan (1992, 1998, 2002), the proponent of this theory, describes a cult based on the goddess of birth, death and resurrection as the main religious practice in Predynastic Egypt. He argues that iconography of this bovine goddess is manifested in the female figurines with raised arms, and states that women in Neolithic and Predynastic Egypt could have been connected ritually with cattle and cattle herding (Hassan 1992, 314). Other evidence used to support his theory is the proposed ritual link between women and water, which Hassan sees in the tattoos or markings on some female figurines from the Predynastic (Hassan 1992, 315; Hassan and Smith 2002, 59). Hassan (1998, 105) argues that these symbolic psychological associations from the early religions of Predynastic Egypt created the later Dynastic Egyptian religious symbolism of resurrection, death and the afterlife. Wilkinson (2003, 15) contributes to this theory by pointing to evidence from the Sahara around 7000 BCE, when cattle may have been venerated even before its domestication.

Hendrickx (et. al. 2009, 215) builds on Hassan's theories and likewise associates the curved raised arms of the El-Ma'mariya figurines with bovine horns, suggesting its connection with bull symbolism. He compares the physical anthropomorphic objects with painted human figures on D-Ware pottery, and argues that the characteristics of both are combined with bovine and bird elements by Predynastic artists and craftsmen (Hendrickx 2002, 283-291). The raised arm motif, often used in D-Ware decoration, and much more rarely in figurines, indicates military or religious power to Hendrickx, and he considers it to be of great significance in Predynastic iconography (Hendrickx et. al. 2009, 212). He also links the raised arm gesture to mourning processions, ritual and sacrifice (Hendrickx et. al. 2009, 212). However, the funerary context of these objects is rarely discussed in his work when constructing these interpretations. A further theory proposed by Hendrickx links unprovenanced figurines with remnants of painted designs to a later Pharaonic group of women musicians of the 'Acacia House' who were associated with hunting (Hendrickx et. al. 2009, 213). Hendrickx (Hendrickx et. al. 2009, 213) suggests that these figurines could be representations of the early version of the Dynastic 'Acacia House' female performers, even though the period of time between these objects and the later phenomenon is quite long.

Eyckerman and Hendrickx (2011a) also conduct a detailed study of Predynastic tusks and tags, producing a number of theories about their meaning and function. They note the presence of tusks and tags in sets in Predynastic graves, but argue that they were stored especially in this way, and therefore had no relation or association to any other objects (Eyckerman and Hendrickx 2011a, 523). Part of this work will test this assumption by examining the placement of tusks and tags in graves in relation to other objects. Additionally, Eyckerman and Hendrickx (2011a, 529) reject the idea that these objects may have been used for body or clothing adornment, but due to the presence of wear on the objects they allow for the possibility that they were not simply used for funerary purposes, but may have been constantly hand-held and manipulated in daily life. Eyckerman and Hendrickx (2011a, 533) sum up their construction of the meaning of tusks and tags by emphasising two main symbolic themes in Predynastic iconography: the female symbolic theme is a combination of human, bovine and bird elements, with the tapering legs having a connection to the so-called 'Naqada plant'. The male symbolic theme is established through hunting as the ultimate masculine, powerful elite activity, to which, Hendrickx and Eyckerman (2011a, 535) argue, tusks and tags are exclusively related. The female symbolic iconography related to female figurines, on the other hand, has the fertility and rebirth in the afterlife and the combination of all these elements together signifies protective power in the Predynastic (Eyckerman and Hendrickx 2011a, 535).

Hendrickx and Eyckerman (2012) construct complicated theories to interpret ritual and artistic expression in Predynastic Egypt, arguing that the best evidence to support the interpretation of bovine horns as upraised arms is the reasoning that Predynastic artists did not have a conception of realism, but operated with abstract combinations of overlapping imagery and ideas to create iconography. Building on their ideas, other scholars suggest that such incorporation of bovine iconography into death and ritual practices shows a more profound link with the political, social and economic aspects of the life in the Predynastic, leading on to connect cattle cult practices with the later iconography of the Narmer palette and state formation in early Dynastic Egypt (Wengrow 2011, 98). Hendrickx and Eyckerman, however, focus more on the discussion of the wide-encompassing symbolic and iconographic themes rather than their context, with the aim to lead their interpretation to explain the state formation of Dynastic Egypt through the development of iconography and pictorial evidence, without specifically identifying the objects' function or meaning.

2.5 PREDYNASTIC MORTUARY STUDIES

As this study will be focused principally on the objects' burial context, two important frameworks will be considered in detail: the study of Predynastic cemeteries and burials, and the study of mortuary archaeology and funerary ritual. Numerous studies and analyses concerned with Predynastic burial practices have been conducted to date, and for the purpose of analysing the gender, wealth, rank and social status of the Predynastic people who were buried with anthropomorphic objects it is necessary to refer to the available sources on this topic. Key studies in this area include those by Bard (1992, 1994, 2001) who has also made a considerable contribution to our understanding of differentiation in burials by identifying the frequency with which certain items appear in Predynastic graves by conducting extensive surveys of several Predynastic cemeteries. Other key studies include those by Stevenson (2009b, 2011, 2013) who analysed the social and ritual characteristics present in a variety of Predynastic burial sites, in order to better understand Predynastic burial customs and culture. Other important studies of Predynastic cemeteries include Castillos (1980, 1982), Anderson (1992), Savage (2000), Friedman (2008a, b) and Wenke (1991). Broader studies of the theory of burial archaeology (Chapman et. al. 1981; Parker Pearson 1982, 2003; Ucko 1969) and of anthropological funerary practices theory (Binford 1971; Turner 1982; Van Gennep 1960) can enhance the study of Predynastic burial practices by providing theoretical frameworks for mortuary analysis. The work will draw on some aspects of these works in order to construct the necessary methodological frameworks for analysing Predynastic burials and grave goods.

As a starting point, a conceptual framework for analysing the dimensions of wealth and social status in burials is required. This firstly will involve some definitions of terms. For example, using Richards (2005, 16), *status* refers to specific ranking or level of an individual in a group, community, society or culture; and *elite* (as in, elite social tank) refers to a non-producing group of the population in a society or community that is supported by surplus. Studying burials in terms of socio-economic differentiation will also involve discussing the social inequality which, according to Paynter (1989, 369-70) 'exists when socially distinct entities have differential access to strategic resources...and this differentiation gives those with access the ability to control the actions of others'. The studies of inequality in archaeology in general, as well as in Predynastic Egypt, usually focus on the development of complex society in which social and economic inequality is considered to be the central factor (Richards 2005, 14). Therefore, when applying such studies to Predynastic mortuary data, for example Bard (1997, 2001), it us useful to remember that these theories are formulated with the aim of tracing state formation in early Egypt and are not always focused on the study of burial practices themselves.

In the 1960s, archaeological mortuary analysis received much attention, with emerging discussions about the best methodologies and theories that could be used to interpret mortuary data. The theories developed by Saxe and Binford (Saxe 1970; Binford 1971), sometimes referred to as 'The Status Approach' or the Saxe-Binford Method, have been extremely influential and formed the basis of many subsequent analyses of mortuary data produced in the last decade. The Saxe-Binford method became, and still remains the standard guideline to conducting archaeological mortuary analysis. This approach relies on the premise that status held by individuals in life will be reflected directly in their burial. Burial variability was taken to reflect variability in society itself (Saxe 1970; Binford 1971; Brown 1981; Chapman et. al. 1981). Tainter contributed further to the ideas of Binford and Saxe by introducing the concept of energy expenditure, reflected in the size and structure of the grave itself, which became another criterion that could potentially measure the rank and status of the inhumed individual (Tainter 1978, 136).

Building on these ideas, several influential works have been produced focusing specifically on Predynastic Egyptian mortuary data (Bard 1994; Savage 1997; Anderson 1992). Bard's work is particularly prominent, as it is sometimes used as a partial guide on the specific analysis of wealth in Predynastic graves. Bard conducted an important study of two large Predynatic cemeteries, Naqada and Armant, in which she outlined a useful framework for analysing Predynastic graves. She constructed a wealth index based on the number of reoccurring objects in the graves she analysed, grouping objects into categories of 'most' and 'least' occurring (Bard 2001, 61, 89). This index may allow identification of rare or luxury items in the graves of the database constructed for this work. An additional statistical analysis of possible correlations (for example, sex of the figurine and sex of the body or links between figurines and other objects and materials in the grave) will be conducted, based on the completed catalogue, in order to determine any significant patterns relevant to the function of anthropomorphic objects in burials.

2.6 THE SOCIAL PERSPECTIVE

The methods proposed by Saxe and Binford, and utilised by Bard and many other Predynastic scholars are relevant in contributing to the analysis conducted in this study, as well as to the study of Predynastic mortuary practices in general. However, new theories have been emerging since the success of the Saxe-Binford method, which approach the study of burials from different perspectives. Significant work has been done by Stevenson (2007a, 2009a, 2013) specifically on the study of Predynastic cemeteries, following the works of other proponents of alternative mortuary analysis perspectives (Hodder 1982; Pader 1982; Parker Pearson 1982, 2003). Many criticisms have since been proposed to the Saxe-Binford method and it is now generally agreed in the field of funerary archaeology that a more cautious approach is needed. Firstly, it has now been acknowledged that burials do not simply reflect social and economic circumstances of individuals and are much more complex. Inversion and distortion of reality occur during burials: 'In death people often become what they have not been in life' (Hodder 1982, 168). It is possible also that 'differences in burial ritual energy expenditure could occur among individuals who do not differ in social importance' (Brown 1981, 411). Indeed, there may be additional great energy expenditures which occur in the form of rituals or ceremonies that are invisible in the archaeological record (Richards 2005, 57).

Alice Stevenson's ideas on conducting mortuary data analysis are highly useful to the study of Predynastic anthropomorphic objects, since she focuses heavily on social relationships and the aesthetics of burials. The approaches Stevenson adopts in her analysis of Predynastic funerary objects and rituals will form the main conceptual framework for this work, especially when analysing the placement of anthropomorphic objects in graves. Stevenson (2009a, 182) challenges the perpetuated assumption that grave goods directly reflect wealth and social status, arguing that since grave goods are most likely selected and placed in the grave by the family and relations of the deceased, direct ownership of the objects may not even belong to the grave owner. Likewise, she challenges the interpretations of unusual or imported materials as luxury items, as well as their relation to the wealth and social status of the individual, but suggests as a possibility that these objects may have belonged to the deceased because of the reverence and respect that person received in the community for their connection to the distant land the object came from (Stevenson 2009a, 187). Part of the analysis will constitute an examination of the grave goods themselves, but will steer away from adopting the methods proposed by Bard (2001) of relating the rarity and value of materials and goods to the elite status of the buried individual. Instead, Stevenson's suggestion that unusual or 'luxury' goods and materials can also reflect responsibilities and roles of the individual in the community, or their social involvement and their levels of influence in the community will be utilised (Stevenson 2009a, 187), as well as the notions of aesthetics and display of the dead (Stevenson 2007a, 81). Memory features heavily in Stevenson's (2009a, 182) interpretations of mortuary data – for example, memory of the individual who wore or used the items in life, membership to social groups, or a memory of wider social networks or relations that individuals possessed related to class, kinship, gender, ethnicity, age, or professional and specialised groups. These ideas and concepts will be applied to the study of anthropomorphic objects in the context of the burial, since their importance and relationship to the deceased individual is rarely considered in previous studies.

Stevenson's (2013, 31) analysis of the cemetery at Gerzeh suggests that objects were not placed in graves at random, but arranged in a particular way. There is considerable variation in the placement of objects, which shows that burial rituals were not static or fixed but perhaps varied from region to region, depending on local customs, and also to some extent on individual choice (Stevenson 2013, 37). This in turn suggests that there were no universal set of rules for burial, but rather some general principles, with improvisation from case to case. This is another important concept that will be utilised in the methodological approach of the study of anthropomorphic objects, since they are found very rarely in graves, therefore regional and individual variations existed in the ways anthropomorphic objects were buried and subsequently the way they functioned in burials. This new approach advocated by Stevenson is not a replacement but an addition to the above mentioned methods of mortuary analysis. It broadens the limitations of previous approaches based on quantative measurements, and brings into prominence the emotional, symbolic and personal significances and the variety of social dimensions in burials.

A useful parallel study conducted by Stevenson (2007b) on the significance and value of palettes in Predynastic Egypt is also closely relevant to the analysis of anthropomorphic objects. The crucial innovation that is put forward in this study is the new method of attempting to understand how such objects are imbued with value, both cultural and social. Stevenson (2007b, 148) considers the way material culture and objects are created and passed through a so-called 'life' of their own, and how this phenomenon in itself can prove to be valuable to understanding the object's meaning. Another significant reason why this study is relevant to the analysis of anthropomorphic figurines is their placement. The palettes were assumed to be associated with the graves of women, but were proven by Stevenson to be found in the graves of both sexes (Stevenson 2007b, 153). Similarly to anthropomorphic objects, the placement of palettes in the grave was usually also close to the body (Stevenson 2007b, 154). These factors, as well as the frequent assumption made by previous scholars that palettes were a valued item, found in elite and wealthy graves (Stevenson 2007b, 156), show the resemblance and relevance of the two connected funerary objects. Stevenson's interpretation of palettes highlights the significance of social and personal value that was placed on objects by individuals and the community, as may have been the case with anthropomorphic objects.

Stevenson's work presents an alternative view to the previously proposed understanding of burial practices in Predynastic Egypt, and provides the theoretical baseline for this study, focusing less on iconography, state development, wealth or status in Predynastic graves, and more on the specific context of the objects themselves. The key aim is to examine the objects in the spacial context of the grave, and in relational context to other objects and the body, with the potential view to explore burial practice as an aesthetic performance. Taking this alternative direction in analysing Predynastic anthropomorphic objects will present them in a new light and form a new perspective, possibly producing results and conclusions that will advance our understanding of the cultural, ritual and social meaning and importance of anthropomorphic objects, and ultimately contribute to the wider encompassing discipline of Predynatic studies.

CHAPTER 3: METHODS OF ANALYSIS

3.1 INTRODUCTION

The theories of material culture and material engagement in relation to personhood, identity and gender, as well as the relationship of these concepts to physical objects in archaeological analysis, will form the basis of the methodology. The approach that has been taken in constructing the methodology proceeds in stages, in order to reconstruct the past through the archaeological record. Following the ideas of V. Gordon Childe (1956, 1), who states that 'the archaeological record is constituted of the fossilized results, of human behaviour, and it is the archaeologist's business to reconstitute that behaviour as far as he can and so to recapture the thoughts that behaviour expressed', the analysis of the data collected for this project will move from concept to concept, in order to put this data in context and come to a deeper understanding of its significance.

The theories that will form the background for the data analysis to follow in Chapter 4 are presented and discussed in this chapter, starting with the theory of material culture. The discussion then follows to the theory of material engagement, examining the close links between physical objects and people, and leading directly into the theories of identity and personhood, and the importance of the role material culture plays in shaping individual identities. Two concepts will then be discussed – gender and its relationship with identity and material culture, and mortuary theory and its close connection to material culture in archaeology. The latter half of the chapter will consist of a detailed outline of the catalogue and its categories.

Material culture studies, when applied to archaeological analysis, focus less on the human aspect and its relationship with physical objects and more on the physical things themselves and their development, qualities, agency and power (Hodder 2013, 30). There has been less interest in human and material object relations in recent studies and more in object consumption, value and physical properties. The recent movement of post-processual archaeological theory introduced new ideas about the role of material culture in archaeology. Material culture was now understood to be meaningful and symbolic, and active in constructing cultural reality and social values in physical form (Jones and Boivin 2010, 336). Following these innovations, current studies of material culture seek to emphasise the materiality and physicality of the objects themselves, constructing so-called 'object biographies', and focusing on the physical properties and the role they played in society (Jones and Boivin 2010, 337).

Caple's (2006) guidelines on object analysis will provide a framework for the analysis of the anthropomorphic objects themselves. The main four focal points of analysis for the methodological framework (physical attributes, decoration and design, value and identity) will be discussed in detail below. However, it is important to remember that such concepts as value, identity and ownership are often interchangeable and intertwined, forming a part of a complex and often contradictory study of material culture. These qualifiers are separated somewhat artificially, and must be seen both individually and as part of a whole physical object.

3.1.1 PHYSICAL PROPERTIES

The nature of a material object is intrinsic to its first and main quality – its materiality. Objects are not simply abstract signs or symbols; they are physical manifestations of ideas in a social and cultural world (Boivin 2004, 64). The first attribute, therefore, that one comes in contact with when looking at or holding a physical object is its physical appearance. The most important physical attributes include size, shape, material and colour, and all these serve a purpose in embodying a degree of beliefs and symbols of a particular culture at a particular time (Caple 2006, 7). All these physical properties form part of a physical, sensory experience for the interacting audience or individuals. As Gosden (2001, 167) argues, the experiences, thoughts and emotions of people in the past may be lost to archaeologists today, yet it may be possible to examine 'the ways in which they set up worlds that made sense to them . . . available to us through an appreciation of the sensory and social impacts of the objects that formed the fabric of past lives'. These physical properties of material objects, with additional parameters such as texture, weight, shape, durability, rarity and availability of the material, mobility, softness, hardness and size might make the objects more suitable for their proposed function, be it symbolic and metaphorical or practical (Boivin 2004, 65).

When considering Predynastic anthropomorphic objects in this light, physical attributes such as size (generally just large enough to hold in the hand comfortably), shape (often a very stylised representation of the human form, with limbs close to the body for convenience of transportation), material (clay or ivory being the most popular, and possibly the easiest to work into the desired shape), and colour (natural surface, sometimes covered in black, red and white paint) assume much more significance. The examination of these attributes (size, shape, material and colour) in the collected database of Predynastic anthropomorphic objects will form part of the analysis to follow.

In addition to the physical attributes, considering other possible features of the physical object, such as diversity, density of deposits and damage (deliberate or situational) will add to the depth of the physical analysis of the data. Examining the diversity of the anthropomorphic objects in terms of their material, shape, size and style could aid in our understanding of their function in Predynastic graves, and whether every such object had a similar purpose. Likewise, the rarity of these objects could perhaps be reflecting the exclusivity of their use among certain social groups.

Examining the possibly of deliberate and strategic damage of these objects by looking for patterns in the breakage (for example, certain figurines always broken in half, or deliberately broken off limbs) would certainly create a new line of enquiry as to the function of three-dimensional imagery in Predynastic burials where the deliberate breakage could have been associated with ritual activity. Fragmentation could even in some cases signify an end to the object's lifecycle, brought around through deliberate destruction of the identity or social persona of the deceased to whom the object belonged (Bruck 2006, 78). The appearance of objects, however, evolves and develops over time (Caple 2006, 7). This is evident when one examines the gradual development of the visual culture in Predynastic Egypt, which seems to be much more varied and free-flowing in its style during the Badarian period, but assumes a more standardised and conventional shape by the time of the late Naqada III period. It is important, therefore, to consider material culture as not static or stagnant, but always a part of an ongoing dynamic process of cultural, symbolic and iconographic development (Wengrow 2006).

3.1.2 DECORATION AND DESIGN

The design of the physical object can be understood and analysed through what Robb (2015) calls the 'design question'. In order to comprehend the choices made by the maker of the object, one must first ask: 'What do artefacts do, and how do they accomplish their effects?' (Gell 1998). Naturally, aesthetic aspects play some part in the physical form of the object, yet the form is created and shaped to meet functional needs, and is constrained within the context and use of the selected materials, available technology, and social and economic condition and factors (Caple 2006, 13). Design and decoration are two distinct concepts that are nevertheless intertwined together, as decoration is part of the overall design of the object. All decoration is significant when interpreting an object, as even the absence of decoration conveys a message (Caple 2006, 51). There can be many reasons for adding decoration to an object: for example, it may increase its value, or it could signify a particular status or social position, shows affiliation, or enable the object to perform a specific role or function (Caple 2006, 51). Gell (1998, 74), in approaching the subject from an anthropological point of view, argues that 'the world is filled with decorated objects because decoration is often essential to the psychological functionality of artefacts, which cannot be dissociated from the other types of functionality they possess, notably their practical, or social functionality'. Attributes of physical objects, such as material, shape and decoration, have energy invested in them because they are communicative or symbolic features (Knappett 2005, 8). Other aspects, such as colour, may be imbued with particular associations, symbols or emotions (Caple 2006, 13; Gage 1999). Therefore, the choices made by the maker of the object are reflected directly in the object's appearance. This is an important point to consider when examining Predynastic anthropomorphic objects, especially the tusks and tags, since these examples feature repetitive patterns of decoration which were evidently important for the maker to distinguish. Aspects of design will be discussed further in this chapter when addressing the problem of determining the sex of some of these objects.

3.1.3 VALUE

The value of a material thing is what changes it from an object into a commodity. Value of material things is socially determined, and created by people (Renfrew 2004, 26). There are different types of material culture values, in the context of which the object can be considered to be a commodity. Value of use, for example, is determined by the usefulness of the object or tool, based on practical considerations (Caple 2006, 6.)

The appearance of objects, however, evolves and develops over time (Caple 2006, 7). This is evident when one examines the gradual development of the visual culture in Predynastic Egypt, which seems to be much more varied and free-flowing in its style during the Badarian period, but assumes a more standardised and conventional shape by the time of the late Naqada III period. It is important, therefore, to consider material culture as not static or stagnant, but always a part of an ongoing dynamic process of cultural, symbolic and iconographic development (Wengrow 2006).

3.1.4 IDENTITY

The identity of an object can take several forms. It can be a record of the past, carrying and preserving memories into the present and future, and embodying past experiences (Caple 2006, 12). An object can also undertake certain roles in culture, tradition, or ritual, which would reinforce the meanings and practices of that particular culture (Caple 2006, 12). Lastly, objects can be the carriers of knowledge. Appadurai (1986, 41) identifies two types of knowledge that may be embodied in an object: the knowledge itself (be it technical, social or aesthetic) which is associated with making the object; and the knowledge of how to use the object. Some objects have even been describes as having 'lives', 'biographies' or 'histories', in distributing knowledge and memories at various times to various individuals (Appadurai 1986, 41). These concepts are particularly important for interpreting Predynastic figurines and other anthropomorphic objects, as their rarity, diversity, and the personal nature of their placement in the grave could indicate that they were highly valued for their personal connection with the dead. Alternatively, anthropomorphic objects may have carried an important ritual role or knowledge that was either to be passed into the afterlife, or to remain with the dead individual who had exclusive ownership and knowledge rights to the object.

3.2 MATERIAL ENGAGEMENT AND PERSONHOOD

The properties of material objects described in the previous section have a strong relationship with the person who is engaging with the objects, which leads directly into the theory of material engagement.

Renfrew (2004, 23) defines material engagement theory as the examination of the relationship between people and the material world, and the significance and status of material objects. As humans, we require sensory stimulations which we receive from objects with our touch and vision, as well as with the expression of feelings and thoughts, and we are inevitably dependant of material things (Hodder 2013, 38). We understand these objects though our senses and our experiences are complex and subconscious, therefore we are unwittingly giving the objects value through our emotional attachment and physical experience (Gosden 2004, 34). In the world of human interaction and social relationships such emotions and attachments play a key role, especially on a personal level, and therefore there is a benefit to considering human emotion as being part of understanding material culture (Gosden 2004, 34). There is a much deeper meaning to be gained through understanding how the material and the social spheres are interconnected, which adds significance and depth to the interpretation of archaeological data, particularly in a funerary context.

Familiar physical things form part of our identity. In archaeological contexts, it is frequently possible to see the elements of identity or various identities distributed and expressed through grave goods (Crossland 2010, 392), as in the case of anthropomorphic objects. These artefacts, which are often seen in the light of indicators or expressions of wealth, power and prestige, are more likely to represent complex combinations of collections, gifts and relationship markers between the deceased and the living (Thomas 2000, 656). Returning to the idea of objects having 'lives' or 'biographies', it is evident that biographical objects form part of a person's identity. Hoskins (1998, 24) argues that people seek to assemble and narrate their life through collections of objects significant to them. Life accounts of people are concentrated on the creation of an autobiography of the self through the vehicle of an object, and are arranged into an identity (Marshall 2013, 209).

Another two significant types of objects that form part of personhood are gifts and heirlooms. The difference between gifts or heirlooms and commodities lies in the greater attachment to and more meaningful associations with gifts (Gosden and Marshall 1999, 172). Strathern (1988) proposed the idea that gifts produce social relations and are active in a mutually creative relationship between people and things. 'People are not just multiple, they are also distributed' Strathern states (1988, 173). A person, in the context of their burial especially, is composed of all the objects they have made and transacted, as well as the objects they have received from others, and these objects are a reflection of a unique identity. Similarly, heirlooms can also form part of a person's identity, especially in burial. Heirlooms in archaeology are objects that have been in the family for several generations, and their value is created through many years of association with various individuals and families (Woodward 2002, 1040). With the addition of objects that could signify prestige, authority or social power, all these artefacts, when placed in a grave, form in some part the identity of the dead. Of course, it is important to remember that the collection, organisation and placement of grave goods were arranged by the family and friends of the deceased, which inevitably detracts from a clear picture of the identity of the dead individual (Bruck 2006, 325). A burial is ultimately the embodiment of what others make of our identity, and not self-expression. We must consider the artefacts deposited with the dead not necessarily as a reflection of the self, but as an expression of the relational nature of human identity, as it is the relationships with friends, kinsfolk and neighbours, and with significant places that made the dead who they are (Bruck 2006, 325).

Ultimately, the data set that forms the main enquiry of this study certainly qualifies for an analysis that takes into consideration the understanding that grave goods are not random artefacts, but objects that could represent part of a person's identity distributed though the grave goods to linger in the afterlife. Such a consideration is particularly relevant for interpretation of human figurines and other anthropomorphic objects.

3.3 OBJECTS AND MORTUARY ARCHAEOLOGY THEORY

An introduction to the main elements of mortuary theory and a comprehensive literature review has already been given in Chapter 2. This section will specifically discuss the methodological approach undertaken in this study in analysing mortuary data. Using examples from Stevenson's work, the methodological framework will centre on the premise advocated by Stevenson (2009a) that Predynastic burials are not necessarily direct reflections of wealth and status of the deceased individual. The examples include Stevenson's alternative interpretation of a large collection of beads in grave 133 at the Predynastic cemetery at Gerzeh as a display of social groups, indicating the individual's interpersonal relationships in the community (Stevenson 2009a, 185). Particular attention will be given to the arrangement and placement of objects in graves in the data analysis, as the close proximity of the object to the body of the deceased is significant, and could indicate a close personal connection (Crubezy et. al. 2002, 473). The aesthetics of arrangements of graves and tomb display will also be given consideration in the analysis, following the ideas outlined by Stevenson (2007a). For example, the placement of particular objects in particular spots might have carried significance, as Stevenson (2007b) argues in her case study of Predynastic stone palettes. Examples of these include palettes being places specifically in front of the body, usually near the hands and the face (this placement pattern appears to be particularly frequent for tusks and tags also). Stevenson (2013, 29) argues that this must have carried significance, since these objects could technically have been placed anywhere else in the grave. Using these ideas the placement of Predynastic anthropomorphic objects in graves will be closely analysed in order to detect any repeating patterns, or any reoccurring associations and relationships with the deceased.

3.4 SEX, IDENTITY AND MATERIAL CULTURE

The relationship between objects and gender is particularly significant to the study of human figurines in Predynastic graves. Figurines with discernible sex are representations, and this is in itself an interpretation of a reality or an element within many constructions of one of many realities (Bailey 2013, 244). In discussing prehistoric figurines, Bailey (2013, 245) states that 'every act of representation is a statement (intentional or casual, conscious or subconscious) that interprets a reality through the dimensions of a particular medium'. This is important to consider when analysing the relationship between the dead and the three-dimensional human representations found with them in their graves, as the physical three-dimensionality of human figurines allows a certain type of engagement for the person encountering the figurine. Engaging with human-shaped objects like figurines may have opened up conceptualization of the role of the body in defining a person, and figurines may in turn be representing the cultural contemplation of the contemporary community of what it means to be female, male, or human in a particular time and place (Bailey 2013, 252).

An additional consideration when examining the relationship between gender and Predynastic human figurines is the status of women and how it is displayed in Predynastic burials. Savage's study (2000) of the social status of women in Predynastic Egypt formed on the basis of the analysis of burial data from Cemetery N700 at Naga-ed-Der, and how it relates to the sex of the individual buried, examined the availability of social roles for both men and women.

The study shows that valuable items were buried with both sexes in equal numbers and in similar places on the body (Savage 2000, 83), and that burials may indeed have been a representation of social roles and identity during life (Savage 2000, 85). The results of Savage's study indicate that women could fill all social roles available to men, in addition to the opportunity to assume a larger variety of exclusively female roles (Savage 2000, 87). It seems plausible that the function of figurines in the burials of both men and women could have been quite similar, that is the function of figurines in burials was not based on the sex of the deceased.

3.5 THE CATALOGUE

In order to document, categorise and present the data collected for this research, a detailed catalogue was put together (see Appendix I), the contents of which will be discussed in the analysis section in Chapter 4. The catalogue forms an integral part of the methodology design, since it helps present the data visually in order for patterns to be identified and for the data analysis to be carried out with ease. The data itself was collected from various sources, mostly from excavation reports, museum catalogues and Petrie's later published notebooks.

The catalogue consists of each object, numbered 1 to 118, laid out vertically against 11 categories. General information about the object can be found in categories one to four: Type of Object, Date, Location and Grave. Individual details of each object are included in categories of Material, Sex of Object, Condition of Object and Position of Object in the Grave. Details about the grave the object was found in are recorded in categories of Sex of Associated Body/s, Grave Condition and Associated Objects and Materials. Each of these categories will now be discussed in detail.

3.5.1 TYPE OF OBJECT

The 118 Predynastic anthropomorphic objects recorded in the catalogue have been classified into six types, which are generally used to classify these objects in Predynastic studies: *Figurine* (objects that clearly retain the human figurine shape), *Tusk* (carved hippopotamus tusks, either solid or hollow, with anthropomorphic features and usually perforated at the top), *Tag* (amulets characteristic of Naqada II, with carved anthropomorphic features, usually decorated with grooves and notches and occasionally perforated), *Comb* (hair combs shaped surmounted with anthropomorphic figures), *Vessel* (pottery with figurative, three-dimensional anthropomorphic decoration) and *Fragment* (parts of objects, often fragmented so badly that it is impossible to determine their sex or original shape).

3.5.2 DATE

Dates have been provided where possible in this catalogue, following the original matrix devised by Petrie's (1901), consisting of 50 Sequence Dates (SD), numbered between 30 and 80 (Dee et. al. 2014, 320). Following Petrie's chronology, Predynastic culture has been divided into three distinct time phases: Amratian or Naqada I (SD 30-37), Gerzian or Naqada II (SD 38 – 60), and Semainean or Naqada III (SD 60 -75). This system has undergone many revisions over the years (Kaiser 1956, 1957; Hendrickx 1996, 2006) and there have also been recent revisions of radiocarbon dates that have been assigned to these cultural periods (Hassan 1985, Dee et. al. 2014). However, for the purposes of this project it is enough to establish the rough timeframe outline. These dates have been rearranged and updated through many studies and are currently accepted to be approximately for Naqada I (4000 – 3800 BC), Naqada II (3800 – 3600 BC) and Naqada III (3600 – 3300 BCE), filling the gap between the Predynastic and the First Dynasty of the Old Kingdom (Bard 1994, Hendrickx 2011, Stein 2011).

The time limit that has been allocated for this particular collection of objects extends between the late Naqada I (approx. 3900 BCE) to the end of Naqada II (3600 BCE).

3.5.3 LOCATION

The objects have been found at 12 different cemeteries in Upper Egypt (see Map, Figure 1). The location category of the catalogue reveals the frequency with which these rare objects appear in various cemeteries. This in turn could indicate potential places of manufacture, or at least where in Upper Egypt these objects appear to have been used the most.

3.5.4 GRAVE NUMBER

The number of the grave has been recorded for every object. In some instances, several anthropomorphic objects have been found in the same grave.

3.5.5 MATERIAL

All the objects have also been categorised in detail according to the type of raw material they are made from. The types of recorded materials range from ivory, vegetable paste (modelled with or without a reed core, and sometimes painted in black, red or white) and clay (also modelled with or without a reed core, and painted). Other materials include limestone, greywacke, shell, gypsum and siltstone.

3.5.6 SEX OF OBJECT

Where possible, the sex of the human figurines will be identified as Male or Female. If the figurine is fragmented and no sexual organs or cultural indicators of sex (such as a clear beard or a small waist and wide hips) can be identified, the figurine's sex will be categorised as Unknown. Tusks, tags and combs usually have very little in the way of identifiable sexual male or female characteristics, and this makes the task more difficult. The methodological framework that will be used to inquire into this issue will be discussed below, in section 3.7, 'Determining the Sex of Tusks, Tags and Combs'.

3.5.7 CONDITION OF OBJECT

The condition in which the object was found has also been recorded in the catalogue. The more detailed descriptions of the object's conditions could include being whole (all body parts present); broken in fragments (small fragments only); broken (only upper or lower body remaining); broken (only the head or separately attached wig remaining). Recording these details could aid in the investigation of the possibility that some of the objects may have been broken deliberately.

3.5.8 POSITION OF OBJECT IN THE GRAVE

This category records the position of the object in the grave, if known. The different placements can be separated into several smaller categories. These include: In a Container (pot, vessel and basket); With Objects (clearly placed in association with another object or a group of objects); Found on Body (object was placed directly on the body); Tied with Leather (applies to tusks and tags only); Found At Hands/Feet/Skull/Between Bodies; Found in the South/North/East/West Section of the Grave.

3.5.9 SEX OF ASSOCIATED BODY OR BODIES

The sex of the body or bodies found in the grave has been categorised to include Male, Female, Child or Unknown subgroups.

3.5.10 GRAVE CONDITION

The condition (whether it is intact, plundered or disturbed) of each grave containing anthropomorphic objects has been recorded in the catalogue.

3.5.11 ASSOCIATED OBJECTS AND MATERIALS

Every item that appears to have been associated with an anthropomorphic object in question has also been recorded in Appendix III. These items range from other anthropomorphic objects to containers (pots, baskets), palettes and mace heads, to name a few. Naturally it has been impossible to record items that may have been taken out of the tomb due to plundering; therefore with most tombs we must assume that the record is incomplete.

3.6 DETERMINING THE SEX OF TUSKS, TAGS AND COMBS

While determining the sex of Predynastic figurines is generally a straightforward task, doing so for tusks, tags and combs is much more complicated. In order to develop a working method and establish possible criteria for identifying sex in these three types of objects, both provenanced and unprovenanced anthropomorphic objects, including some that have not been added to the catalogue, will be used for comparative purposes. Additionally, in studying and comparing the tusks, tags and figurines together, rather than in separate groups, some new light may be shed on the ways Predynastic peoples may have identified and depicted sex, and what importance they may have assigned to it.

Tusks present a less complicated issue in identifying their sex. All known Predynastic tusks date between late Naqada I to Naqada II periods, and their design and decoration usually falls into two distinct types (labelled Type 1 and Type 2 in the catalogue). Type 1 tusks (example: Figure 2), only one of which is provenanced and included in the catalogue, are usually surmounted by an intricately carved head with a distinctive beard. Type 2 tusks (examples: Figures 31 and 33) are much simpler in design, with only rough outlines of human features carved into their surface. It is plausible that Type 1 tusks can be identified as male, due to the apparent beard they are depicted with. However, all comparative material depicting bearded men, including palettes, knives and statues such as the MacGregor Man, dated to later Naqada II and Naqada III periods (Harrington 2004, 2006; Nowak 2004, 894), making for a time discrepancy in comparison.

Similarly to tusks, tags can be subdivided into three categories. Type 1 tags (examples: Figures 42, 43 and 44) are flat, rectangular-shaped tags, with a groove at the base, Type 2 tags (example: Figure 68) are smaller with tapered-down bases and perforated at the bottom and Type 3 are the pin-tags (examples: Figures 7 and 35), tapering down, with a narrow waist and wide hips. The Type 3 tags have been classified as figurines in the catalogue. The sex of tags belonging to Types 1

and 2 is almost impossible to define, since very little detail is given to the definition of the object's sex in its design, even though it is very clear that they do represent humans. The tags of Type 3 are more detailed and complex, and require attention to detail in the interpretation of their sex. For the purposes of this work, the sex of all tags of Type 3 and some tags from the Type 1 category will be considered to be female, for the reasons outlined below.

Opinions as to the sex of these pin-like tags differ. Eyckerman and Hendrickx (2011a, 527) argue for the sex of all tags to be male: 'The female aspect is completely lacking, despite the fact that female representations are frequent among Predynastic figurines. As far as gender is involved in the tusks and tags, it is exclusively related to masculinity.' The major reason for Eyckerman and Hendrickx's identification of the sex being male is the depiction of the pointed chin or 'beard' in the tags' anthropomorphic imagery (Eyckerman and Hendrickx 2011a, 527). However, both Nowak (2004, 896) and Brovarski (2005, 215) consider it possible that the pin-tags are female. If the pointed chin, considered by Eyckerman and Hendrickx in every case to be a beard, is seen as an exaggerated elongated chin, it is then possible to see the pin tags, with their accentuated narrow waists and wide hips as female. Indeed, a female figurine from grave B109 (Figure 26) at Abadiya, dating to Naqada II, has a clearly elongated, pointed chin but also prominent breasts, wide hips and a narrow waist. In this case it is clear that a female figure could be depicted with a pointed chin rather than a beard. Alternatively, the pointed chin could be depicting something altogether different – perhaps the pin tags are depicted wearing the famous Hierakonpolis clay masks, which have prominent pointed chins and ears (Adams 2002, 2004). Such masks may have been worn by both men and women (Figure 99).

Several other points can be made to support the suggestion proposed here that the pin tags are in fact depicting the female form. Firstly, almost every example of pin tags, both excavated and purchased, is depicted with decorative patterns or dots around their necks, perhaps to show necklaces. If the artist wished to depict these patterns on the chest area, the inclusion of protuberant breasts would have been an encumbrance. It is possible that breasts were deliberately omitted from pin tags for this practical reason, since they would be inconveniently placed for the dotted decoration to be applied, and a flatter surface would serve much better for that purpose.

Secondly, it is evident that time, energy and labour went into shaping the pin tags' pointedly narrow waists, when it may have been easier to leave them smooth or squared off in shape, like the Type 1 and 2 tags. Therefore, there was clearly a deliberate intention to depict the waists and the wide hips in order to indicate the female form.

Thirdly, pointed chins may not necessarily be depicting beards on pin tags, and therefore may not be a solid indication of masculinity, as can be seen in the example of the Abadiya figurine with a pointed chin and breasts.

And lastly, to bring in a final piece of relevant evidence which will be discussed in detail in Chapter 4 and Chapter 5, tags were found in the graves of both men and women. As they may have been used by both sexes it is not unreasonable to suppose that they were not exclusively associated with masculinity, and may have depicted both men and women.

3.7 DATA ANALYSIS

The main purpose of the database was to arrange the data in an organised way in order to facilitate its analysis to identify any cross-tabulate patterns. The design of the analysis in Chapter 4 is based on the catalogue data and the organisation of the catalogue described above. The analysis will follow a six-point outline, with the aim of gaining better understanding of the reasons for anthropomorphic objects being placed in Predynastic graves, and what their function might have been.

The first line of enquiry will examine the variety of ways in which objects were placed in graves. The category of object placement will be used to provide information and to identify possible repeated patterns of placement, detecting the specific placements that were preferred for specific objects. For example, tusks and tags tied with leather, or figurines placed directly on the body. The context of anthropomorphic objects has been briefly discussed by Ucko (1968, 177), who commented that these 'are bound to be of interpretive interest'. However, as Ucko's (1968, 178) analysis only covered a small selection of figurines and excluded all tusks and tags, there is some room for an addition to the inquiry he previously began.

The second line of enquiry will examine the range and combinations of different grave goods that have been found in graves in connection with the anthropomorphic objects, as well as examples of multiple depositions of anthropomorphic objects in the same grave. The aim is to trace any materials or objects that are repeatedly associated with anthropomorphic tusks, tags, combs or figurines in Predynastic graves.

The combination of the sex of the anthropomorphic object and the sex of the body the object is associated with will form the third line of enquiry. The questions that this particular analysis will attempt to answer are: 'Is there a visible relationship between the sex or type of the object and the sex of the body?' and 'How frequently can such a relationship be identified in the graves?'. This issue has already been briefly raised by some scholars, mainly when relating to the placement of tusks and tags in the graves of women (Eyckerman and Hendrickx 2011a, 521; Podzorski 1993, 124) and this analysis will attempt to determine how significant such a placement is in the interpretation of the function and meaning of these objects. The aim is to spot all possible relevant patterns and document the frequencies with which the patterns appear.

The type of material from which the anthropomorphic objects are made will be analysed in the fourth line of enquiry. It is already becoming evident from collecting the data that the chosen

material depended on the type of object being made. For example, almost all figurines were made from clay or vegetable paste, and all tusks and tags from hippopotamus ivory. Furthermore, certain materials have been suggested to be associated with the sex of the object, in particular the association of vegetable paste with female figurines (Eyckerman and Hendrickx 2011a, 2011b; Hartung 2011). The aim, therefore, is to determine whether there is in fact a definite preference in material for the different types of objects, and whether the choice of material was indeed associated with the sex of the object.

The fifth line of enquiry will focus on studying any possible object breakage patterns. Previous studies by Chapman and Gaydarska (2007, 2009) examining deliberate breakages in figurines will be used as a guide in order to determine if there is a real possibility that these objects were broken deliberately when deposited in the grave. The types of breakages will also be analysed, to see whether there was a systematic pattern or if the breaks occur at random. Lastly, the sixth line of enquiry will examine a unique occurrence which emerged during the collection of the data. Several anthropomorphic objects have an almost identical copy placed in a different grave; therefore an apparent link between the two graves seems to be evident. This particular occurrence will be given more attention in Chapter 4.

3.8 PROBLEMS AND DIFFICULTIES

There are several problems that the proposed methodology design will inevitably encounter and attempt to overcome, and it is important to now acknowledge these. The major issue is unfortunately the lack of data – every effort has been made to accurately collect and catalogue all available data for the chosen period between late Naqada I and Naqada II, and yet only a few of the graves recorded in the catalogue are intact. Most graves are either disturbed or plundered, leaving the data record incomplete. Furthermore, the records of grave excavations are often incomplete or missing, and some of the anthropomorphic objects themselves have also been lost. Sometimes, when a description of the anthropomorphic object is given, or the sex of a body is identified, there is no certainty that the description or identification is correct or reliable.

The period selected for this study, as has been mentioned before, spans roughly 600 years, from the late Naqada I (approx. 3900 BCE) to the end of Naqada II (3300 BCE). However, it is important to remember that anthropomorphic objects were made before and after this period. Indeed, the division of the Predynastic timeline into periods, while useful for many reasons to archaeologists, detracts from the natural passage of time and the natural development and change that took place during the whole extent of the Predynastic period. Therefore, placing the chosen selection of Predynastic anthropomorphic objects into this wider context allows for a deeper and more accurate interpretation of the said selection.

In terms of the objects themselves, the most significant issue is their rarity. Out of thousands of Predynastic graves dating to the period between Naqada I and Naqada II, only 59 tombs contain anthropomorphic three-dimensional objects. Many of the objects themselves are in very poor condition, sometimes with only small fragments surviving. In addition to the data that has been collected here, which only included anthropomorphic objects found in graves from the specific timeframe, there is a collection of similarly provenances objects found in a settlement context. These settlement sites include several figurines from El-Badari (Brunton and Caton-Thompson 1928), figurines in Naqada south town (Zawaydah) (Di Pietro 2011) and Amra (Hill and Herbich 2011), a figurine fragment from Aidama and several fragments in the settlement of Hierakonpolis (Friedman 2013, 7).

There is also a vast body of unprovenanced data, including a large collection of unprovenanced ivory figurines, which Ucko has studied in detail to develop a way of dating them (Ucko 1965). Even though this data is unusable for the purposes of this study, when discussing the extreme rarity of Predynastic anthropomorphic objects, and the singularity of the methods of their deposition, one must acknowledge the many unprovenanced examples, or those coming from settlement contexts. In most cases it is impossible to detect the exact location, date and even on occasion authenticity of unprovenanced anthropomorphic objects (Ucko and Hodges 1963). Yet it is possible to conclude that this type of object, though appearing to be extremely rare when judging from the provenanced collection, may not have been as rare as the provenanced data indicates. Some examples of unprovenanced figurines seem to be almost exact copies of provenanced figurines: two figurines from graves B109 (Figure 26) and B83 (Figure 16) from Abadiya bear a striking resemblance to a figurine (Figure 95) from the Museum of Art, Rhode Island School of Design, and two figurines (Figure 96) placed in a stand at the Ägyptisches Museum und Papyrussammlung Staatliche Museen zu Berlin. Therefore, it is reasonable to assume that more Predynastic graves may have originally contained anthropomorphic three-dimensional objects than can now be ascertained.

Anthropomorphic objects have very rarely been found in settlements; however, there are several prominent examples. These consist mainly of figurines - such objects as combs, with known locations, all come from funerary contexts (Alvarez and Rosales 2004, 885). Tusks and tags are also mostly found in burials, with very few found in settlements like El-Badari (Eyckerman and Hendrickx 2011a, 518). Four settlement figurines come from the Badarian period (approximately 4500 BCE – 4000 BCE) – two from El-Badari (Brunton and Caton Thompson 1928, Pl. 24, 25, 55), and two from Mostagedda (Brunton 1937, Pl. 40, 42). The exact context and position of these four figurines, however, is unknown. The only other collection of figurines to come from a settlement context is an additional group of four female figurines that have been excavated in a settlement area at El-Mahasna, and have been dated to the late Naqada I to early Naqada II period (Anderson 2011, 18-19). They were found in settlement deposits at the ritual structure in Block 3, with one figurine found broken and scattered in fragments around the area, and some additional 54 fragments recovered in the general vicinity (Anderson 2011, 18-19). It appears as though the figurine was deliberately broken apart and scattered, perhaps as part of a ritual (Anderson 2011, 18). These anthropomorphic objects, though extremely rare in their context, provide an additional view of their possible interpretation. The fact that they do not come from the funerary context may indicate the possibly that such figurines had various purposes in the day-to-day life, and may not necessarily have been intended for funerary deposition.

There are 12 cemeteries in total in which graves with anthropomorphic objects were found, presenting a great variety of location. The largest amount of object and of graves are present at the Naqada cemetery (41 objects, 23 graves), which could indicate either a centre of production or simply the main location where anthropomorphic objects were in use. It is significant that almost all anthropomorphic tags (except for five from Matmar) come exclusively from Naqada, even though non-anthropomorphic tags are plentiful in most other Predynastic cemeteries. It is a similar case with anthropomorphic tusks and combs. There are only six anthropomorphic tusks and three anthropomorphic combs, yet four tusks and all three combs come from Naqada, and only two tusks come from Badari, again with many numbers of non-anthropomorphic geometrically carved tusks and undecorated and animal-shaped combs to be found in many Predynastic graves in general. Out of the large collection of 110 Predynastic combs analysed by Alvarez and Rosales (2004), only 5.7% were considered anthropomorphic. In terms of tusks and tags, both decorated and plain, 571 in total come from a known provenance (Eyckerman and Hendrickx 2011a, 498). Unprovenanced tusks and tags which can be considered anthropomorphic are much more numerous, but in total there are 67 known anthropomorphic tags and 57 known anthropomorphic tusks, both provenanced and from unknown locations (Eyckerman and Hendrickx 2011a, 502).

For the purpose of conducting a thorough and detailed analysis, an additional collection of graves, which can be found in Appendix II, will be included in some parts of the analysis in Chapter 4. This is a group of intact graves in which non-anthropomorphic tusks, tags or combs have been placed. The placement of these objects, even though they are not decorated with human imagery, has survived undisturbed, and therefore the inclusion of this group of graves in the analysis could give us more information and insight into object placement, when the number of intact placements of anthropomorphic objects has proven to be so small.

CHAPTER 4: ANALYSIS AND RESULTS

4.1 SUMMARY OF THE DATA

The total amount of three dimensional anthropomorphic objects dating to late Naqada I and Naqada II periods, analysed and compiled in the catalogue (Appendix I), is 118, and the total number of graves is 59. Anthropomorphic objects are categorised into four main types: figurines, tusks, tags and combs. A fifth category (vessels) only contains a few rare examples of either vessels made into a human shape, or a vessel surmounted and decorated by three-dimensional human figurines.

Figurines and figurine fragments are the most numerous among all the object types: there are a total of 56 figurines and a further 31 fragments of figurines with an excavated provenance from this period. Female figurines and fragments certainly appear more frequently (there are a total of 42 female figurines) whereas male figurines and fragments only number 13. Fragments form the second largest group of objects, numbering 31 individual fragments, some of which may come from different graves and some from the same grave. This is the case with grave 186 from the El-Ma'mariya cemetery, which contained six separate figurine fragments. From the total amount of objects collected for the database, figurines and figurine fragments number 87 objects out of 118 in total, approximately 74%. The total amount of female objects is 52 (44% of all objects); male objects number 15 (13%) and the sex of 51 objects (43%) is unknown (see Table 1).

Anthropomorphic tusks and tags signify a much smaller proportion of objects comparatively - there are only six tusks and 20 tags in total. Non-anthropomorphic tusks and tags (those with simple geometric line designs or completely unadorned surfaces) are very numerous in this period and are found in many Predynastic graves. The carving of the human image on these types of objects, however, seems to have been quite rare – anthropomorphic tusks and tags constitute 22% of the total amount of all anthropomorphic objects. Non-anthropomorphic tusks and tags are much more numerous in Predynastic graves, which is a possible indication there was a preference for geometric or plain designs of these objects rather than for human imagery. In order to supplement the rarity of anthropomorphic

TABLE 1: NUMBERS OF OBJECTS PER TYPE

	FEMALE	MALE	UNKNOWN/ NO SEX	TOTAL
FIGURINES	42 (75%)	13 (23%)	1 (2%)	56 (100%)
FRAGMENTS	4 (13%)	1 (3%)	26 (84%)	31 (100%)
TUSKS	0	1 (17%)	5 (83%)	6 (100%)
TAGS	4 (20%)	0	16 (80%)	20 (100%)
COMBS	0	0	3 (100%)	3 (100%)
VESSELS	2 (100%)	0	0	2 (100%)
TOTAL	52 (44%)	15 (13%)	51 (43%)	118 (100%)

objects, to provide an additional body of data to the very scarce records of object placements in graves especially, and to felicitate better understanding of the patterns of these placements, an additional appendix comprising 12 graves from four different cemeteries (Mostagedda, Matmar, Naqada and El'Mahasna), and containing in total 25 non-anthropomorphic tusks, tags and combs has also been included in some of the analysis sections. For the full list of additional graves, see Appendix II.

In terms of location, the scarcity of data prevents the possibly of a more solid conclusion, but there is evidently a pattern connecting anthropomorphic combs, tusks and tags to the location of the Naqada cemetery. In terms of anthropomorphic figurines, the cemeteries of El-Mahasna, El-Amrah and Abadiya contain considerable amounts of objects and graves with anthropomorphic objects, compared to only one grave and one object from the cemetery at Qau, two objects from one grave at Ballas, and two objects from two graves at Mostagedda. This indicates that at certain locations in Predynastic Egypt anthropomorphic three-dimensional imagery was produced and utilised more frequently than at others.

4.2 DETERMINING SEX OF ANTHROPOMORPHIC OBJECTS

The determination of sex in figurines has been previously discussed in more detail in Chapter 3. In the data presented in the catalogue, female figurines are classified as female by the presence of either breasts or the pubic triangle, with additional consideration of the narrowness of the figurine's waist. Male figurines are classified as male by the presence of the loincloth or codpiece which outlines the male genetalia. For some figurines no images are available, therefore the decision regarding their sex has been made on the basis of the description provided by the excavator. This is the case for objects 13, 16, 18, 19, 21, 22, 23, 24, 25, 26 and 30 (See Appendix IV).

The sex of tusks and tags is rarely evident and there are several examples, such as the three tags from grave 276 at Naqada, which have incisions on their chins possibly indicating a beard. However the four tags from grave 2682 at Matmar must be considered female, according to the methodological approach used in this work, outlined in Chapter 3. The smallest number of objects comes from the Combs and Vessels categories – three combs and two vessels in total. One of the combs could be male, due to the possible hairs indicated on the elongated chin; the other two could arguably be female, following the previously outlined methodology in Chapter 3 of identifying sex, but since the waist of the figure is not depicted, it is also impossible to know definitely. All the objects classified as vessels are female or associated with female figures. Therefore, the numerically largest category of objects with anthropomorphic imagery is the figurines, followed by tags, and the rarer tusks, combs and vessels.

4.3 PLACEMENT OF OBJECTS

Since only 24 of the 59 collected graves (only 40%) have a record of the placement of grave goods, the additional appendix collection of graves with known placements of non-anthropomorphic tusks and tags has been separately included, in order to attain a clearer picture of the results (see Appendix III). With this extra addition, the amounts of objects whose place in the grave is known, compared to those with unknown placements, can be calculated. The placements have been compiled on the basis of calculating every single object – for example, every one of the four anthropomorphic tags found in grave 2682 at Matmar is included in the category 'In Container', as opposed to collectively counting them as one item. From all figurines and fragments, only 30 have known positions, and 56 are unknown; 11 tusks have a known position and two are unknown; 22 tags have a known position and 10 are unknown; seven combs have a known position and two are unknown; and only one of the two vessels has a known position. This amounts to the total of 71 out of 118 objects with known positions in the grave.

CHAPTER 4: ANALYSIS AND RESULTS

Table 2: Placement of Anthropomorphic Objects in the Grave

	TOTAL	WITH OR NEAR BODY	IN CONTAINER	LOCATION IN GRAVE N/S/E/W
FIGURINES	30	17	5	10
TAGS	10	2	6	3
TUSKS	4	2	1	1
COMBS	1	1	1	0
VESSELS	1	0	0	1

The different types of placement of anthropomorphic objects in the graves can be divided into three categories: objects in close proximity to the body (for example, near the hands or feet, or directly in front of the body), objects placed in a container (pot, basket, etc.) and objects deposited in specific areas of the grave (sometimes in combination with other objects). These categories often overlap – for example, a figurine from grave 3740 at El-Badari was found in a basket laid on the chest of the female body buried in the grave, thus fitting into two separate categories (In Container; Near the Body). This overlap is reflected in the results shown in Table 2.

It is evident from the results in Table 2, in the case of tusks, tags and combs in particular, that the data is scarce and fragmented. It would be extremely difficult to form any conclusions or even suggestions as to the possible meaning of this data and the significance of these placements when so little information is available. On these grounds it has been decided to supplement the available data of anthropomorphic tusks, tags and combs with an additional collection of non-anthropomorphic tusks, tags and combs whose position in their graves has been recorded (see Table 3). As provenanced non-anthropomorphic tusks, tags and combs appear much more frequently than the anthropomorphic kind, it is justifiable that this data is relevant and can be used to provide additional information about the possible patterns of placement of these objects, and subsequently about their function in Predynastic graves.

Placement close to the body is the most frequent (47 out of 71, 66% of all objects with a known placement), and reoccurs often with figurines and tags especially. Indeed, 56% of figurines and 68% of tags are found close to the body. Less frequently, objects are found in vessels or baskets. A reoccurring combination here is an object placed with a group of other grave goods into a container, and then placed in a certain area in the grave (as in grave 72 at Hierakonpolis, or grave 271 at Naqada). Anthropomorphic objects are also frequently found in a separate area of the grave, usually placed there with a collection of other objects. This was undoubtedly deliberate, but with a possibly that some objects may have been displaced from their original position due to plundering or grave disturbance. Tags and figurines are also most frequently found in containers. However, these numbers owe much to the availability of data, as there are more tags and figurines with known placement than tusks, combs or vessels.

Table 3: Placement of Non-Anthropomorphic Objects in the Grave

	TOTAL	WITH OR NEAR BODY	IN CONTAINER	LOCATION IN GRAVE N/S/E/W
NON-ANTHRO TUSKS	9	7	0	2
NON-ANTHRO TAGS	13	13	5	0
NON-ANTHRO COMBS	6	5	1	0

Table 4: Placement of All Combined Objects in the Grave

	WITH OR NEAR BODY	IN CONTAINER	LOCATION IN GRAVE N/S/E/W
FIGURINES (30)	17	5	10
TAGS (22)	15	11	3
TUSKS (11)	9	6	3
COMBS (7)	6	2	0
VESSELS (1)	0	0	1
TOTAL (71)	47	24	18

Table 5: Placement of Objects near the Body

	Figurines	Tusks	Tags	Combs	Non-Anthro Tusks	Non-Anthro Tags	Non-Anthro Combs
Near the Head	7	-	-	-	2	2	2
In Front of Body	1	2	2	1	5	2	1
Behind the Body	4	-	-	-	-	-	-
Laid on Top of the Body	2	-	-	-	-	5	1
Near the Feet	2	-	-	-	-	-	-
Near the Hands	1	-	-	-	-	5	2

The most useful and comprehensive placement category seems to be that of placement close to the body, since more than half of the objects can be categorised into it (see Table 5). The detailed results from this category indicate that figurines were most frequently placed near the head of the body or behind the body. The preferred placement of tags is near the hands, whereas tusks are most often placed directly in front of the body. Combs, contrary to what would naturally be assumed, are not only found close to the head, but are also often found near the hands or in front of the body.

Table 6: Relationship between Placement and Sex of the Body

	In Container	With/On Body	Area in the Grave
Female Body	2	10	-
Male Body	4	-	1
Child Body	1	-	
Male/Female in One Grave	1	1	4
Unknown	4	7	13

A further analysis of the type of placement and associations with the sex of the buried body suggests possible correlations (see Table 6). The preference in graves with male occupants seems to have been to place the anthropomorphic objects in a container, as four out of five graves with male occupants display this placement type. While these are indeed small numbers, and a more robust sample would have been desirable,

the pattern is still clear. In graves with female occupants, the preference seems to be to place the object on the body – objects from 10 out of 12 graves with female occupants are placed this way. For graves with several occupants of both sexes, objects are rarely associated with one specific body, and instead are frequently deposited in a separate area in the grave.

4.4 OBJECT GROUPINGS

This section of analysis and results will cover the patterns that can be found in the deposition of groups of anthropomorphic objects compared to only one object placed in a grave. Additionally, an analysis of the types of other objects and materials that are often found with anthropomorphic objects will be conducted. For the completion of this analysis, for the same reasons outlined in section 4.3 of this chapter, the groupings of the additional collection of non-anthropomorphic tusks and tags (Table 9, also see Appendix II) will be used to supplement the scarce data collected for the anthropomorphic tusks and tags.

In terms of figurines, the placement of only one figurine per grave, both for male and female figurines, seems to have been preferred, and a few examples of female pairs of figurines are also evident (see

Table 7). Tusks are almost never places singly in one grave, but are nearly always deposited in pairs or groups. Often one of the tusks would be non-anthropomorphic, while the other would be carved with anthropomorphic imagery, or one would be solid while the other one hollowed out. The grouping of tags into 1, 2, 3, 4, 5 or more tags in one grave is much more variable, with no clear preference (see Tables 8 and 9).

TABLE 7: FIGURINES PER GRAVE

	1 PER GRAVE	2 PER GRAVE	3 PER GRAVE	4 PER GRAVE	5+ PER GRAVE
FEMALE FIGURINES	14	5	1	-	2
MALE FIGURINES	5	1	-	-	-

TABLE 8: ANTHROPOMORPHIC TUSKS AND TAGS PER GRAVE

	1 PER GRAVE	2 PER GRAVE	3 PER GRAVE	4 PER GRAVE	5+ PER GRAVE
TUSKS	1	6	-	1	-
TAGS	2	2	2	2	2

TABLE 9: NON-ANTHROPOMORPHIC TUSKS AND TAGS PER GRAVE

	1 PER GRAVE	2 PER GRAVE	3 PER GRAVE	4 PER GRAVE	5+ PER GRAVE
TUSKS	-	1	1	-	-
TAGS	2	1	3	-	-

4.5 OBJECT ASSOCIATIONS

Anthropomorphic objects, especially those placed in containers; seem to be associated with a range of other grave goods and materials. All the objects found in the nine selected graves have been recorded and grouped into 42 different categories (see Appendix III).

For the purpose of obtaining results on the anthropomorphic objects having any possible associations with other objects in the grave, and to discover whether the Predynastic graves contain anthropomorphic objects displaying any particular patterns in their inventory of grave goods, nine graves (eight intact and one partially intact) have been selected from the catalogue to form a database for this analysis. The choice of the eight intact graves, with the addition of the partially intact grave H.41 from El-Mahasna, was made deliberately, since all other graves in the collected catalogue have been disturbed or plundered and it would therefore be impossible to ascertain their original contents and form an accurate analysis of said contents. Grave H.41, even though partially plundered, was included due to the fact that it is the largest grave in the catalogue, containing the largest amount of goods out of every other recorded grave with anthropomorphic objects. A large variety of objects was found in each grave, including pottery, beads and palettes among other frequently occurring objects, while their quantity varied from grave to grave.

Out of all raw materials, resin seems to be most frequently associated with anthropomorphic objects, being found placed together with them in eight different graves. Malachite is also similarly found, in six different graves. Occasionally, a palette, often accompanied by a grinding pebble, is found together with anthropomorphic objects – this can be seen in five different graves. And very occasionally, mace heads are found in association, in two separate graves.

The graves themselves provide some visible detail about the complete mortuary collections of objects that would have appeared in many Predynastic graves (see Appendix III for details). Graves, such as grave 3165 from Badari, grave 1832 from Mostagedda, and graves H.29 and H.41 from El-Mahasna contained at least one or two and often a variety of ivory objects. These included bracelets, cowries, combs, tusks and tags. Most graves also contained some type of pottery (rough, red-polished or black-topped). Interestingly, all but one grave (H.41) contained a palette, and some graves contained two (graves 3165, H.29, T4 and 72), often shaped differently and varying sizes. No other objects appear with the same frequency as palettes in these graves, yet some types of materials and goods recur consistently in some of the graves. Among these objects, mace heads appear in four graves, shells in four graves, and collections of pebbles in four graves. Beads of carnelian or steatite also appear in the same three graves, and flint tools and

flakes, in one case a collection of 34 separate stone tools (grave 72 at Hierakonpolis) have been found in four different graves. Bones of a variety of animals (goats, sheep and cows) were found in five graves. Materials such as limestone, wood, matting and basketry also make a frequent appearance – matting is found in two graves, basketry in two graves, limestone in four graves and wood planks or fragments in three graves.

There are also objects and materials that occur much more rarely – these include gold, silver, ostrich egg shells, leather, lead ore, sulphate of lime, calcite and grain. These only occur once out of nine cases. Additionally, four of the nine graves contained some very unique objects, including 83 fossilised nummulites in one grave, game board and pieces, mussel shells and burnt organic matter, and a fabric pillow with a variety of plant remains. It is appropriate in this instance to turn to Bard's 1994 study, where the topic of rare goods is touched on in regards to differentiation of rank in Predynastic burials. Group 1 of Bard's frequencies of grave goods in the Armant cemetery, which includes goods that appear only once or twice, lists Natica shell and red ochre – materials that occur once and three times respectively in the nine intact selected graves (Bard 1994, 60). Group 2 includes items that appear three to five times, which occur in the selected graves, including calcite, ostrich egg-shell and resin (Bard 1994, 60). Calcite and ostrich egg shells are found in one grave, and resin is found in six out of the nine graves.

Bard (1994, 61) identifies 65 materials in total in the study and states that "the presence or absence of rare materials in graves might be a valid basis for differentiation". This is indeed possible, and Bard makes a compelling case, yet with such a small sample as has been presented here and the nature of this project being more focused on the social and personal functions of anthropomorphic objects, grave differentiation is not possible to ascertain or be certain of. In terms of associations between anthropomorphic objects and other objects in the graves, although certain materials and items do occur consistently, with malachite and resin often found prominently close to anthropomorphic objects themselves, there are otherwise no strong indications of any particular patterns. What can be seen is a distinct diversity of unique objects and a lack of standardisation of the burial item collection.

4.6 RELATIONSHIP BETWEEN SEX OF THE BODY AND SEX OF THE OBJECT

For this part of the analysis, figurines have been separated from tusks and tags in order to specifically determine the likelihood of correlation between the clear figurine human image (possibly resembling the owner of the grave) and the sex of the grave occupant (see Table 10). Unfortunately, much of the data needed to conduct this analysis is unavailable, due to the rarity of the records of the sex of the bodies. However, with the data that is available, it is possible to perceive that there is an indication of a pattern between the female body and the female figurine. Additionally, the sex of all figurines placed in children's graves (where possible to determine) appears always to be female.

In a separate comparison, anthropomorphic tusks and tags, including the additional graves with plain examples, are grouped together in order to determine whether they are normally placed in the graves of men, women or both (see table 11). In this case, the indications are slightly clearer – the majority of tags appear in graves of women, and tusks seem only to appear in the graves of women. This, however, is possibly due to the lack of data, since for most graves containing tusks, the sex of the occupant is unknown. In this instance, the additional collection of non-anthropomorphic tusks, tags and combs (Appendix II) has been used to supplement the results and examine the relationship between the type of object and the sex of the body (Table 12), in the hopes of attainting some clearer patterns in the course of the analysis.

4.7 OBJECT MATERIALS

Anthropomorphic three-dimensional objects are usually made from three main materials – clay, vegetable paste, or ivory (see Table 13).

TABLE 10: RELATIONSHIP BETWEEN SEX OF THE BODY AND SEX OF THE FIGURINE

FIGURINE SEX	MALE BODY	FEMALE BODY	MIXED SEX	CHILD BODY
MALE	3 graves	2 graves	2 graves	-
FEMALE	1 grave	5 graves	1 grave	3 graves
UNKNOWN	4 graves	1 grave	-	2 graves
TOTAL	8 graves	8 graves	3 graves	5 graves

Table 11: Anthropomorphic Tusks, Tags and Combs from Male and Female Graves

	FEMALE BODY	MALE BODY	UNKNOWN
TUSKS	2	-	7
TAGS	10	4	12
COMBS	-	1	3

Table 12: Non-Anthropomorphic Objects from Male and Female Graves

	FEMALE BODY	MALE BODY	UNKNOWN
TUSKS	-	-	3
TAGS	5	-	1
COMBS	1	1	2

Table 13: Materials of Objects

	IVORY	CLAY	VEGETABLE PASTE	OTHER	TOTAL
FEMALE FIGURINE	6 (12%)	37 (75%)	6 (12%)	1 (2%)	50 (100%)
MALE FIGURINE	2 (16%)	10 (77%)	1 (7%)	-	13 (100%)
FIGURINE FRAGMENTS	4 (16%)	18 (75%)	2 (9%)	-	24 (100%)
TUSKS	6	-	-	-	6
TAGS	12 (60%)	-	-	8 (40%)	20 (100%)
COMBS	3	-	-	-	3
VESSELS	-	2	-	-	2
TOTAL	33 (28%)	65 (55%)	9 (8.5%)	9 (8.5%)	

The preference of material for human figurines, both male and female, was normally clay, with occasional use of vegetable paste – 65 figurines and fragments in total are made from clay, which makes it approximately 75% of all figurines. Human shaped vessels are also made from clay. A small number of figurine examples are made from ivory, but only female figurines tend to be incised with black paste, while ivory male figurines are plain. Only nine figurines and fragments are made from vegetable paste, which constitutes only 10% of all figurines. There does not seem to be a preference for material based on the sex of the figurine, therefore it can be assumed that no one material exclusively belongs to one sex.

An interesting feature of both clay and vegetable paste figurines is that they are frequently painted, especially the facial features. Out of 87 figurines, 57 are painted (approximately 65%) either in red (20 objects), black (five objects), white (22 objects), or with a combination of black, white and red (six objects). Red and white seemed to be the more popular colours – figurines were either completely coated in red paint (haematite) or their lower bodies were painted white to indicate a skirt, as can be seen in the famous example of the El-Ma'mariya figurines (Figures 72 to 93).

Tusks are always made from hippopotamus ivory, naturally being the tusks of that animal. All three anthropomorphic combs collected for this catalogue are also made from ivory, although in general combs are made from both ivory and bone. The majority of tags (60%) are made from incised ivory. The remaining 40% are made from a variety of stone types: four are made from 'slate' or greywacke, three from plain stone and one from alabaster.

4.8 OBJECT BREAKAGE PATTERNS

Figurines are rarely found intact – most have some kind of evident breakage. Only 20% of female figurines have remained intact. Male figurines are more frequently found whole – 60% of them are intact.

It is uncertain if the breakage is deliberate, or is simply due to natural causes. For example, if a fragile small object like a figurine was to break due to age or disturbance, the head and arms would be the weakest points and would almost certainly break off. However, there does appear to be a breakage pattern for female figurines – 44% are broken off in the middle, with only the lower body remaining in the grave, and the upper body missing completely. There are other examples, particularly figurines and fragments from grave B101 from Abadiya and grave 1705 at Naqada, where it is evident that the elongated lower limbs of the figurine were broken up into several pieces, and in the case of grave 1705, only one piece has remained in the grave. Schematic drawings (Figures 100 and 101) show broken figurines grouped together.

4.9 SIMILAR OBJECTS IN DIFFERENT GRAVES

There are five cases of nearly identical anthropomorphic objects being found in two different graves. All five of these cases come from the Naqada cemetery, with the total of 10 graves. The first example is in graves 271 and 1757 (Figures 40, 62 and 63). Grave 271 contained one and grave 1757 contained two tags – all three look remarkably similar to each other, and are made from the same materials (slate with inlaid shell). Example two is from graves 276 and 1583 – both contained an ivory incised human tag. However, while the tag in grave 276 was whole and intact, the tag in grave 1583 was cut in half, with only one half deposited between the two bodies buried in the grave, whose sex is unknown. Graves 1546 and 1788 provide the next example – both contained small identical looking clay wigs that would

TABLE 14: OBJECT BREAKAGE

	HEAD ONLY	LOWER BODY	TORSO	HEAD BROKEN OFF	INTACT	TOTAL
MALE FIGURINE	-	-	-	4	8 (60%)	13
FEMALE FIGURINE	1 (2%)	22 (44%)	5 (10%)	12 (24%)	10 (20%)	50

have been attached to the heads of human figurines (grave 1546 contained two figurine wigs – Figures 54 and 55; grave 1788 contained one – Figure 65). The next example is from graves 1411 and 1561 – an identical looking human-headed comb (Figures 45 and 56) was found in both graves, with the only difference being that one of the combs was double-sided (Figure 45). The last example is from the two famous graves at El-Ma'mariya (grave 2 and grave 186) and grave U502 at Abydos. In all three graves examples of very similar looking female figurines were found (Figures 70 and 71; Figures 73 to 93). All had white painted lower bodies to indicate skirts, distinctly shaped pointed faces and resin residue in the back of the heads where a wig would have been attached. However, the figurines from Abydos were surmounted on the edge of a vessel, all 8 of them holding hands (Figure 70). Furthermore, three other male figurines of a similar style were found in grave U502 (Figure 71), and were clearly used to decorate the rim of another vessel, but have since been broken off, accidentally or on purpose. In all these cases, the majority of the bodies are missing or of unknown sex. Only graves 1546 and 1788 have occupants of known sex – a child was buried in grave 1546 and an adult male in grave 1788.

Similar objects, especially figurines or objects with anthropomorphic imagery, originating from different graves appears to be a rare phenomenon in Predynastic Egypt. Excluding such examples as palletes, which were clearly replicated to a similar style and therefore look similar to each other depending on the chosen designs, there are several other examples from graves at Abadiya. Graves B86 and B83 (included in the catalogue) both contained very similar looking animal figurines. Additionally, several human figurines from graves B109 and B83 (Figures 16 and 26) have identical looking unprovenanced counterparts (Figures 95 and 96) although it is not clear whether they were removed from the same graves and later sold.

CHAPTER 5: DISCUSSION

5.1 INTRODUCTION

Most scholars, when considering the subject of Predynastic human imagery, use the iconographic approach. Eyckerman and Hendrickx (2011a), in their detailed study of Predynastic tusks and tags, explain how, in their view, the interpretation of such objects should be made:

> 'When attempting to understand the meaning of these enigmatic objects, we should not so much focus on their possible use, since we do not have the necessary information, but rather on the concepts that may lie at their origin, as reflected through formal elements. (Eyckerman and Hendrickx 2011a, 529)'

Such an approach it valid and extremely valuable to our understanding of the function of these objects, especially as there is such an abundance of anthropomorphic iconographic imagery appearing not just in three dimensional forms but as decoration on all sorts of objects in the Predynastic period. The context of anthropomorphic objects usually plays a relatively small part in their interpretation in most recent studies, mostly because it is generally considered that there is not enough data available. Furthermore, and as Ucko had done a partial analysis in 1968, a further study into the burial context of these objects is generally considered unnecessary. However, it has been the aim of this study to inquire into this subject and to conduct a thorough investigation of the graves with anthropomorphic objects, which makes this particular study a somewhat unique deviation from the standard approach.

In keeping with this alternative approach to the data, the methodologies of figurine studies from other ancient cultures have been taken into account and used where possible, in order to present a new outlook and to produce accompanying results as to the function of three-dimensional imagery in Predynastic burials. Lesure (2011, 51), in his examination of prehistoric figurines from various cultures, defines several fundamental questions which can be asked of general human figurines from any time or society, to then frame the interpretation of the said figurine. These questions can be applied fittingly to the concluding discussion about the function of Predynastic anthropomorphic objects. Firstly, to address the subject matter of the objects: what did the image depict? This question should be answered separately for figurines, tusks, tags and combs, as it has become quite clear throughout the analysis that each type of objects represents different symbolic and iconographic concepts and has different functions. Figurines, both male and female, seem to represent individuals, as is evident firstly from their placement in extreme close proximity to the body, and in some cases deliberately imitating the position of the body. Figurines most frequently occur singly in graves, and are the most diverse objects in terms of style, design and abstractness. This could be indicating the fact that figurines were shaped by individuals who did not necessarily specialise or were particularly skilled in modelling, although examples like the figurines from El-Ma'mariya show extraordinary and delicate craftsmanship. In most cases, they seem to have been made by or for the deceased individual, and represented either the actual individual or people related to them. If deliberate breakage is taken into consideration, figurines may have been a further vessel for memory and personhood connections, where fragments of the figurine remained in the grave, with other fragments being presumably taken and kept by friends and relatives. It is entirely possible that the figurines had further functions in everyday life. For example, figurines may have been used in rites of passage, where the figurine was later kept by the individual to memorialise the event; or as objects associated with certain rituals, and later deposited in the graves of individuals that either engaged in or led such rituals in the community. Altogether it seems that figurines were more personal items, imbued with a deep, more emotional meaning or memory for the buried individual.

Tusks represent an altogether different image. They seem to form part of a collection rather than represent a personal memory or image for an individual. In graves, tusks always occur in groups, are frequently tied together, and are very rarely carved with human images. This also applies to most tags. It is possible on the basis of the context analysis, to form an image of their function that is quite separate from that of Predynastic human figurines. Tusks are collected items, treasured as possible hunting trophies or prized and sought after objects in general. It is interesting to note that they occur most frequently in the graves of women, which seems to contradict the hunting trophy function, even though it is possible that women, as well as men, participated in hunting activities. On the whole, tusks appear to be treasured items, which were possibly collected for prestige, or for magical or ritualistic reasons.

Tags, on the other hand, are much more standardised in terms of design, and much more heavily stylised than figurines. This could indicate that all of them depicted the same subject matter. The most readily acceptable interpretation is ancestor figurines, as this could explain why the design and style of the tags was so repeated and lacked variety, unlike the figurines. Perhaps there was an iconographic standard, understood and accepted by the contemporaries, by which tags were made in order to make them functional ancestor representations. It is possible that if they were rendered and carved in a certain way, they would then be imbued with protective or healing powers, or some other ritualistic or symbolic function. The case of the small tag from grave B33 at Hierakonpolis (Figure 68) being found in a basket among what appears to be paraphernalia of a witch doctor or healer illustrates this point particularly well.

Tusks and tags seem to share many traits in terms of their context – both are often tied together, both are more frequently carved with similar geometric designs, both have traces of leather which indicates they were suspended and worn, and both are more frequently found in the graves of women. It is difficult to account for these characteristics, and the shared features of two such different types of objects. But nevertheless it is reasonable to assume that these objects were somehow related either in function or subject matter or both. One very obvious connection is the material they are both made from – hippopotamus ivory and incised black paste. Tags are occasionally made from a variety of other materials, but it could be suggested that these objects may have been occasionally carved by the same people. Combs and vessels on the other hand are very minor object groups, and appear to be unique decorative anomalies, rather than falling into a function category of figurines, tusks or tags.

In drawing attention to the possible meanings of anthropomorphic objects at certain cemeteries, it is important to likewise focus on the general rarity of such graves and objects in Predynastic Egypt. The occurrence of anthropomorphic objects, though varying in numbers from cemetery to cemetery, nonetheless remains extremely rare. For example, Petrie (1901, 32-34) states that the cemetery of Abadiya, described by him as one of the largest and best cemeteries he recorded contained up to 570 graves. However, only five graves at the Abadiya cemetery contained anthropomorphic objects, barely 1% of the total amount of graves. Similarly, Ayrton and Loat (1911, 2) estimate that at El-Mahasna 'of the original number of graves in our cemetery would be about six hundred, and of these we excavated about one half, ignoring those which had been too obviously plundered to repay digging again'. Only six graves containing anthropomorphic objects were found at El-Mahasna, which therefore constitutes only 2% of the total amount of excavated graves. Even the cemetery at Naqada, where the largest amount of graves containing anthropomorphic objects out of any cemetery had been found, considering that the total amount of graves numbers over 2,000, the graves with anthropomorphic objects constitute only 1%. Therefore, it appears that anthropomorphic three-dimensional imagery in Predynastic Egypt was very scarce, and did not generally form part of the standard collection of burial goods. The reasons for this will remain unknown; however is it possible to assume that such objects were either buried for particular reasons or special occasions. Rare objects, as noted by Stevenson (2009a, 187) may have been placed in burials to indicate or reflect a particular social role or status of the individual in the community.

This may be the case with figurines in particular, since non-anthropomorphic tusks, tags and combs are frequently present in Predynatic burials. Figurines do not feature prominently in Predynastic burials for a reason, yet it is difficult to determine what this reason might be. Certainly, figurines made from less durable materials may have long since disintegrated in some graves, yet many figurines still survive, sometimes fragmented, left behind in burials that were plundered in antiquity. It is possible that figurines in particular were an especially personal or magical item, perhaps even being somewhat taboo and therefore remained untouched by contemporary grave plunderers. They may have been used more actively in the performance of the burial ritual, yet were not an especially sought after grave good. Alternatively, figurines may have been particularly associated with the individual, being a highly personal item only used by that individual. Therefore, upon their death, an item of such high personal significance may have been passed on to the individual's family or left in their grave to accompany them into the afterlife, depending on the wish of the individual or on circumstance.

5.2 PLACEMENT OF OBJECTS

As can be seen from the results in Chapter 4, there are suggestive patterns in the placements of anthropomorphic objects in Predynastic graves, and clear patterns emerge from the collected data. Unfortunately, only 40% of the excavation records of graves collected for this analysis contains information about the placement of grave objects. This factor makes it necessary to treat results and interpretations of the data with caution; however it is also possible to perceive distinct patterns in the available data.

The types of placements of anthropomorphic objects have been roughly separated into three categories: with or near the body, in a container, and in an area of the grave. In fact, these three categories frequently overlap, especially in the case of tags - the largest amount of tags is found in a container, which is placed on or close to the body of the deceased. The general repeated placement patterns for all anthropomorphic object types seems to be that of placement on or near the body, since they constitute 66% of all object placement methods. As the placement of all object types generally near the body is so frequently repeated, it is reasonable to assume that for anthropomorphic three-dimensional objects this is the placement that was primarily desired, possibly for the reasons of a personal and close connection or relationship between the object and the individual. Ucko (1968, 178), in his original analysis of the objects' context states that 'figurines...placed on the skeleton, may be evidence of a special relation between the figurine and the deceased...[and] may also suggest a special relationship between the deceased and the figurine'. There seems to be a clear distinction between the placement patterns of figurines and tusks and tags. At first, a cluster seems to appear at the placement of figurines behind the body (see Chapter 4, Table 5); however, all of these figurines come from the same grave, Grave 271 at Naqada, which will be discussed below. The real preferred placements for figurines appear to be near the head or directly on the body, as can be seen in graves H. 41 and H.29 at El-Mahasna (both are the graves of women in this case). In the first, the figurine is laid directly on the body and moulded to resemble the shape of the body; in the second, fragments of figurines are placed behind the head of a female body. Moreover, figurines placed thus are rarely found in a container, unlike tusks and tags. The only exclusion from this pattern is the figurine found in a basket of resin, placed on the chest of a female body in grave 3740 at El-Badari.

Lastly, figurines, more than any other type of object, are found in areas around the grave. This could be due to deliberate placement away from the body, as an additional object to supplement the grave good collection, with no particular relation to the individual. Or alternatively it could be due to disturbance and plundering of the grave itself. Yet, when looking at the details of the placements, the former option seems more probable – six figurines (all from the plundered grave B101 at Abadiya) were found in the north area of the grave, which bulks up the clustering of these results. Additionally, two further examples

– a fragment in the intact grave H.42, and a whole ivory figurine grouped with four tusks at the intact grave H.29, both from El-Mahasna, signal a deliberate placement, rather than a disordered and strewn object collection left behind by grave robbers. Another example is the clay female figurine (Figure 39) in grave 271 at Naqada, which was deposited in the north area of the grave, with the collection of other objects (rather rare for figurines), while four other female figurines were placed in a line in front of the body. These examples seem to point to the possibility that apart from a personal and close placement of figurines along or directly with the body, an alternative placement of figurines in the grave, especially for large groups of figurines, indicated a less personal addition to the group of grave goods.

A particularly unique placement of figurines, though rare, deserves a further scrutiny. Grave 271 at Naqada is the site of a very unique deposition of female figurines – Petrie (1895, 32) describes how 'a row of ivory figures stood upright in the clean sand along the side of the grave, equally distant, and undisturbed'. This grave was plundered, and yet the figurines were left undisturbed. They were placed 'along the east side of the tomb, behind the body's position, placed upright at 3 inches apart...in a bed of clean sand, with sand behind them' (Petrie 1985, 21). This seems to be a very deliberately arranged placement, and what is more, it is not the only one of its kind. The two figurines at the Ägyptisches Museum und Papyrussammlung Staatliche Museen zu Berlin (Figure 96), which have been mentioned before as resembling a figurine from grave B83 at Abadiya (Figure 26), were placed in a stand, with room for four figurines to be standing in a row, almost exactly imitating the figurines that Petrie discovered at Naqada. Although these two figurines and the stand are unprovenanced, the resemblance they bear to the figurine in the Abadiya grave indicates that it is almost certain that they are genuine, and may have possibly also originated at Abadiya. This type of placement, apart from being clearly deliberate and also very rare and therefore unlikely to be part of a repeated and common funerary ritual. It seems to reflect particular 'meanings assigned to particular visual encounters' (Hallam and Hockey 2001, 131). The dramatic staging of the body, surrounded by 'props' such as these figurines, placed in a row, arranged by friends and relatives, bring the individual back to life through material culture, with enduring memories for the survivors (Hallam and Hockey 2001, 130).

Additionally, the placement of objects in a row in a clean bed of sand indicates a specific and deliberate choice made by the relatives and friends of the individual who would have arranged the burial. Such a placement may in fact have been of ritual significance, requiring very specific conditions and arrangement. It may also have formed part of the burial performance, staged during the burial of the deceased by the community. The figurines are clearly on display for people to see. The exact meaning of such a deliberate display is impossible for us to understand today – all we can see is a tantalising glimpse into the burial practices conducted in Predynastic society, which seem to have been quite distinct, but also varied from case to case.

Ucko (1968, 428) notes in the section of figurine placements in the grave that 'it is necessary to stress that, assuming the figurines have different functions, the particular place of any individual figurine in the tomb or particular sex of figurine and skeleton concerned may be significant'. Bearing this in mind, the variety of the figurines themselves, in combination with the evident variety of established preferences of their placement in the grave certainly does seem to indicate a variety of function and meaning associated with the figurine's look, material, style and placement. For instance, figurines like that in grave H.41, placed directly on the body, and shaped to resemble the form and pose of the body itself, could be conveying a personal and intimate relationship between the figurine and the buried individual.

The rare and striking example of four figurines placed in a row behind the body may reflect a different meaning and function, possibly closer in nature to the figurines placed in the areas further away from the body, which seems to be symbolising different meanings and associations. Perhaps the figurines were arranged to support, protect or guide the individual into and in the afterlife. There is no clear demonstration of a close bond of the figurine with the body, as is evident in the other examples, and the figurines do not seem to be directly related to the body. Instead, these more distant figurines have been placed either more formally and imposingly in a row, almost observing the body of the buried individual, perhaps representing ancestors, prominent kinship ties, prominent community individuals or even deities. The figurines placed further away or added to the objects collected in the grave would have, on the other hand, formed part of the material accompaniment of the dead, possibly to support and assist the dead into the afterlife.

The placement of tusks and tags in the Predynastic graves, although seemingly similar, does differ significantly from the placement of the figurines. The placement of tags seems to concentrate near the body and especially at the hands, whereas tusks are most frequently found directly in front of the body. One particular placement, which Nowak (2004, 899) considers to be the tags' proper position in the grave, is that of tags laid out along the forearm of the body. This placement is relatively common and appears in graves B75 and A88 in El-Amrah (MacIver and Mace 1902, 24, 36-37) and in grave G75 from Mahasna, which is included in Appendix II. These objects are also, more than any other type of object, placed in containers with other objects and materials to form part of a collection or set of other tags or tusks and a variety of objects and materials. This can be seen, for example, in the case of the grave B333 at Hierakonpolis. There are enough differences and similarities between the placements of tusks, tags and figurines to warrant the supposition that these object types may have had specific separate functions, as well as a possible general overarching and simplified meaning that could have been common to all Predynastic anthropomorphic objects and well understood by contemporaries in whose graves these objects were eventually placed.

In terms of positioning relating to the sex of the body, there are also some evident patterns and differences. There are very few examples of placements with male bodies or children, and defining patterns in these placements proves to be very problematic. The really distinct pattern worthy of notice is the frequency with which anthropomorphic objects were placed directly with female bodies – most anthropomorphic objects found with female bodies were placed on or very near the body, as were the only two examples of objects in female graves found in a container, in both cases a basket (grave 3740 at El-Badari and grave A.57 at El-Amrah). In grave 3740 the figurine in the basket was placed on the chest of the body, and as grave A.57 was plundered, it is possible that the original placement of the basket could have been similar.

The placement of objects, and not just of the anthropomorphic kind, in these burials appears to be closely related to aesthetics and the concept of burial composition and organisation by the living related to the dead individual, as has been suggested by Stevenson (2007a). One of the intriguing concepts Stevenson (2007a, 77) unravels in the notion of the burial being staged and orchestrated by the survivors. The careful arrangement, with obvious regard for symmetry, balance and composition, appears to be almost a funerary performance, with its remaining striking effect of drama and enactment evident in the placement of the objects (Stevenson 2007a, 79). An additional suggestion of graves being on display to be viewed by the living (Stevenson 2007a, 87), before final internment took place puts such careful and precise arrangements into even sharper focus and provides some reason and clarity as to their chosen position. Stevenson (2007a, 88) notes that the importance of aesthetics in the arrangement of Predynastic burials is clearly identifiable, and was therefore valued as a means of creating an accurate and memorable impression of the deceased individual. Using the same concepts, it can also be argued that the placement of objects in Predynastic burials would have been indicative of their importance to the buried individual, and also indicative of the role they played in the individual's daily life or would play in their life after death.

Deliberate placement of objects in front of the body, especially near the hands and the face, when they could have been placed anywhere else in the grave, has been previously discussed. In general, the reason for such careful placements of objects in prehistoric graves, seemingly full of respect for the dead, as Pollard (2001, 316) argues, '...is not fully explained by their role as components in an orchestrated process of signification, as there is often a certain 'style' to deposition that demands explanation.' It has been noted that not only anthropomorphic objects were placed carefully in particular areas – Stevenson (2013, 29, 35) found in her study of the Predynastic cemetery at El'Gerzeh that palettes and stone vessels were often found placed in front of the body, and similarly, flint knives were often placed in front of the hands and forelegs at the cemetery at Naga ed-Der (Savage 2000, table A7). In addition, certain types of objects are known to have been repeatedly placed in particular areas of Predynastic graves, such as pottery (Stevenson 2013, 31). These examples show that object deposition was carefully planned and orchestrated for every type of object placed in the grave.

The role that aesthetics played was central in arranging a proper and functional funerary ritual, but the practical element was also present. This is especially evident in the anthropomorphic objects placed in containers. Bruck (2004) in an analysis of Early Bronze Age burials in Yorkshire takes note of the objects which were wrapped or placed in bags or containers. Bruck (2004, 319) argues that such placement may have served a protective function, as well as being a means of control. Containment of a selection of certain objects allowed specific artefacts to be grouped together, and at the same time be separated from other objects, allowing for categorisation that would have played a central role in the functioning of mortuary ritual (Bruck 2004, 319). Such separation and containment could have created a successful display of aesthetical theatre that would have prompted the essential sensory responses needed for a successful burial ritual (Pollard 2001, 330). Wengrow (2006, 166) proposes a further view of containers, such as baskets and jars, as framing the spatial boundaries of the burial, and signifying a correlation between the number of containers and other unique or prestigious goods in the grave. The manner in which objects were deposited in graves was likely influenced by many factors, especially by the meanings assigned to objects through their production, use and symbolism (Pollard 2001, 316). A Predynastic burial, therefore, can best be viewed as 'the transformation of the body into an idealised vessel for the containment of social relations' (Wengrow 2006, 165). During the burial, this transformation was played out through the materiality of the objects, their symbolism and according placement in the grave, and the Predynastic funerary rituals were performed and completed with all these elements coming into play.

Based on the results of the analysis of the objects' placements, it can be concluded that there is a definite pattern indicating deliberate placement of anthropomorphic objects. The previously accepted position on placement by many Predynastic scholars that 'overall no regular patterns can be observed' (Eyckerman and Hendrickx 2011b, 425) in the context of anthropomorphic objects can now be challenged and revised by this conclusion. Based on their placement, tusks and tags seem to be less personal, private and intimate in their meaning in the grave, but seem rather to reflect a specific ritual or funerary function. It is possible that, like many other objects placed in Predynastic graves, their function was not strictly related to the funerary ritual, but instead may have served a function in the day to day life, and therefore fill their place in the grave in that capacity. Tusks and tags bound with leather and placed together in groups seem to be reflecting uses that were carried out by the living in daily life. Upon the death of the individual who owned a pair or group of tusks or tags they were placed in the grave in a similar way in which pottery or tools were also placed in Predynastic graves – as a representation of the collection of objects owned and used by the individuals in life and which they or their relatives or friends chose to accompany them into the afterlife.

The situation seems to be different with figurines. As was mentioned before, the intimate nature and deliberate placement of figurines in graves, as well as their greater variety of style, seems to reflect a more fluid meaning and symbolism. This meaning may have been created and dictated by the particular individual rather than the community. Therefore, it is reasonable to assume that the function of figurines and burials may have been meaningful and personal to the individual, and was possibly more significant in the funerary ritual capacity, and less associated with communal and shared daily rituals and concepts. It is indeed possible that the figurines were made individually by the owners, rather than by a skilled craftsperson (as seems to be the case with tusks and tags, due to their relative uniformity).

In the end, it will never be possible to identify the precise meanings and functions of objects from their placements, or even the meanings of the placements themselves. However, as Stevenson (2013, 38) asserts, it is possible 'to recognise the meaningfulness of the activities as materialised in grave structures.' It is clear that the placement of anthropomorphic objects was meaningful, and was meant to convey meaning to those who created it and viewed it. Anthropomorphic objects like figurines, tusks and tags formed part of a 'material language', and Predynastic people were using this language to convey statements, constructing them through association, separation, similarity, difference and deliberate placement (Thomas 2002, 78). It is likewise possible that the placement of these objects was associated with their function, or in some cases even conveyed their function, whether it was practical, symbolic, social or ritual in nature. Gender, rank, age, profession, social standing and the state of death would all have been reinforced by object placements in specific ways and by the spacial relationship between the body and the surrounding objects (Pearson 1998, 39). What is evident is the variety and yet the relative uniformity of such deliberate placements. They may reflect the function of anthropomorphic objects as being both fluid and personal to the individual, and yet a common and overarching function that existed and was known in Predynastic society.

In summary, it is now clear that we can learn much more than had previously been thought about the function of anthropomorphic objects from their placements in the grave. Eyckerman and Hendrickx (2011b, 425), when discussing the significance of context for Predynastic figurines, state that 'the incomplete information on the context of most figurines restricts the possibilities for recognising any specific characteristics of the tombs involved and at present no obvious reasons for the presence or absence of figurines in Predynastic tombs can be proposed'. Contrary to this statement, the results of the analysis conducted in this study prove otherwise, as there are clear indications that figurines and anthropomorphic objects in general did have a place and play a role in Predynastic burial customs, and their presence signified highly personal individual connections of people to anthropomorphic material culture.

5.3 OBJECT GROUPINGS

Anthropomorphic objects, like many other types of objects found in Predynastic graves, are often found in groups of two, three or more. There are distinct differences in such groupings between figurines and tusks and tags. There is a clear preference for a single object per grave for anthropomorphic figurines, especially for female figurines, as 15 graves have a single female figurine. An interesting pattern emerges on closer examination of the female figurines that were placed in groups of two or more. In all but one of the eight graves with more than one figurine, the figurines look very similar to each other, as though they were originally made together, intentionally to resemble each other. A few great examples include two figurines (Figures 49 and 50) from grave 1488 at Naqada, which look almost identical in style, as well as in the places where they were broken. Similarly, grave 394 from Naqada contained two seated female figurines (Figures 46 and 47), again made to look deliberately similar. The most famous example of this pattern is from the two graves at El-Ma'mariya, one of which contained two intact figurines, and the other contained 20 broken figurines and fragments, all of which were female. This last grave seems to be a significant outlier, with the number of figurines exceeding any other graves. However, there is also evidence of dissimilarity between the sets of figurines, the best example of which are the figurines from grave B101, in which every figurine is significantly stylistically different from the rest. Figurines in groups of two or more displayed no significant difference in placement discussed in the section above, although none are found directly on the body or in a container.

Both anthropomorphic and non-anthropomorphic tusks display a strong grouping pattern – they are almost always found in groups of two and are frequently tied together by leather straps. In grave 1419, two anthropomorphic tusks were found together in front of the body tied by leather. Moreover, anthropomorphic tusks are frequently paired up with non-anthropomorphic ones. In both graves 1419 and 226 an anthropomorphic tusk is paired up with a non-anthropomorphic tusk; and in grave T4, the two anthropomorphic tusks were paired with two non-anthropomorphic. Baumgartel (1960, 60) proposed a possible explanation for the pairing of tusks – she noticed that occasionally one of the tusks would be hollowed out, while the other would be left solid, and therefore suggested that one is meant to represent a female and the other a male element. However, not all tusks correspond to this pattern, and there are several known cases were tusks are found in smaller sets of three (Eyckerman and Hendrickx 2011a, 521), therefore this interpretation does not fully match up with the data. Additionally, based on this reoccurring pattern of twin tusks, Eyckerman and Hendrickx (2011a, 525) suggest that graves yielding only one example of a tusk or tag must have been disturbed or plundered. However, the only anthropomorphic tusk placed singly in a grave was found in grave 3165 at Badari, and is additionally the only tusk of its kind, being a Type 1 tusk. Grave 3195 seems to be intact, with many objects recorded as being still in their original places (Brunton and Caton-Thompson 1928, 45-46). There is certainly a deliberate intention to put tusks together in pairs, and occasionally in sets of three, which could be reflecting their function. The deliberate pairings are further reinforced by the leather straps tying the tusks together. There is clearly some kind of symbolic meaning associated with tusk pairs in particular, whether it is related to their function, the way they were used, or originally made together.

The arranged groups of tags appear to be less restricted – there is no continuous pattern of pairs of two, as with tusks. Rather, the pattern of tusks groups is quite evenly spread out between one, two, three, four and five or more, frequently tied together by leather straps. It is clear that tags were meant to be placed together in sets, yet it is difficult to explain why. Nowak (2004, 899) proposes that they possessed a specific function, probably magical in nature. Eyckerman and Hendrickx (2011a, 521) argue that because tags, and also tusks, were tied together, they were never worn on the body – a theory also supported by Baumgartel (1960, 65). However, the way objects were placed in Predynastic graves, while possibly reflecting their function, could also be influenced by aesthetical, symbolic or even practical reasons. Many tags were found singly, placed in containers with other objects, such as the tags from graves 271 and 1583 from Naqada, and the single small tag from grave B33 at Hierakonpolis. The tag from grave 1583 the first one was placed in a basket with malachite and resin, and the second tag from grave 271 was found cut in half vertically with only one half remaining, with tusks, tags and resin. The small tag from grave B33 was found in a basket with a collection of a variety of items, including plant remains, bone tools and amulets. These examples show that tying tags together may not have been the standard or the only way of placing tags in graves. Since tusks and tags are very frequently placed together, and are almost always deposited in sets of two or more, it is possible to imagine that there is some kind of association between them and that they usually perform their function, whether practical or symbolic, in sets. There are several exceptions to this rule, with examples of single tusks and tags, and even one example of half a tag, which displays variety in a sense that no definite and fixed way of placing tags and tusks in graves existed. This could in turn indicate that the function and symbolic association with these objects was equally versatile.

5.4 OBJECT ASSOCIATIONS

Out of the nine intact graves selected for this part of the analysis, none displayed any solid patterns in terms of anthropomorphic objects being associated with specific grave goods or materials. However, there are two minor results that emerged from this analysis that will be discussed. The first is a possible connection between anthropomorphic objects and malachite and resin, in the arrangement of the grave goods. The second feature that ought to be noted is the contents of the selected nine graves in terms of quantity and diversity.

CHAPTER 5: DISCUSSION

The two most frequent materials that appear in graves in which anthropomorphic objects are also found are malachite and resin. Out the nine intact graves, three had malachite and six had resin, almost always found placed close to the anthropomorphic objects. Malachite is a vivid green mineral which occurs in the Eastern Desert and the Sinai Peninsula, and has been used from the Badarian times onwards (Aston, Harrell and Shaw 2000, 43). Malachite is usually either mined as copper ore or ground into powder to be used as green eye paint (Aston, Harrell and Shaw 2000, 44). It has frequently been found in Predynastic graves either on palettes or in its raw material form put in bags or baskets, and preserved as part of the funerary equipment (Aston, Harrell and Shaw 2000, 44). Resin, formed from the sap of a variety of trees, reached Egypt in Predynastic times and would most likely have been imported since there is a very limited quantity of trees in Egypt (Serpico and White 2000, 430). The uses of resin in the Predynastic remain unclear; however it is possible that resin was prized for incense and ointment uses, due to its fragrance (Serpico and White 2000, 430).

Both resin and malachite seem to have had cosmetic or personal uses, rather than practical ones. However, it is impossible to build a satisfying and justified conclusion or theory about the evident frequency with which malachite and resin appear together with anthropomorphic objects. On the broader scale of things these results are not exactly clear, and there is enough room to doubt the intentionality of the placements of these objects with anthropomorphic objects. Further research into the placement of resin and malachite in Predynastic graves in general is required before any conclusions can be reached as to the possibility that these materials are somehow related to anthropomorphic three-dimensional imagery.

The second prominent feature of the nine graves that emerged during the creation of the graves' inventory is the notable presence of a large variety of unique objects which rarely occur in other Predynastic graves. Firstly, not many objects of a practical nature are present in all the nine graves. Instead, a reoccurring feature of each of the graves is the abundance of objects of diverse materials, sizes, shapes and origins. There are several very unique and rare examples: there are 83 nummulite fossils in grave 3165 at Badari, there is a game board with separate modelled pieces in H.41 at Mahasna, there are mussel shells in grave H.29 at Mahasna, and a large variety of plant remains and a fabric pillow in grave B33 at Hierakonpolis. In addition, there is a large quantity of various clay objects present in almost all of the nine graves – there are cup-shaped perforated objects, 'garlic' models, clay cones and rattles. The clay cones have been previously discussed by Eyckerman and Hendrickx (2011a, 517-518), who argue that they have a connection with tusks and tags, and often with hippopotamus figurines. Additionally, there are varieties of shells, beads, ivory objects and raw materials in every one of the nine graves, all of which also have a comparatively large quantity of goods.

It can be reasonably concluded from examining the intact graves containing anthropomorphic figurines that these graves usually also contained a wide variety of other collected objects. However, this does not necessarily reflect wealth, economic superiority or high social status of the buried individual. Although there has been a general movement to disassociate, at least partially, from the established theoretical framework based around the Saxe-Binford method for mortuary studies, there is still an undeniable focus on establishing socio-economic parameters and quantifying variables in Predynastic mortuary studies (for example, Anderson 1992; Bard 1994; Wilkinson 1996; Savage 1997; Rowland 2007). When analysing Predynastic graves, the intention of this study was to step away from such methodologies, as the goal of the analysis is not to confront the idea of anthropomorphic objects in wealthy graves. The focus instead was on determining the function of these objects based on context, placement and the arrangement of the burial and accompanying rituals.

A case study similar to that conducted in this study is that of the Nubian A-Group burials, which examines the difference in status between the graves of women and children (Nordstrom 1996). Nordstrom (1996, 34-35) arrived at a similar conclusion in terms of the social status displayed in the Nubian burials – the emphasis of the study was on diversity, not rank or status. He concluded that vast arrays of personal items were deposited in the graves, displaying the individual's personality and identity rather than their levels of wealth (Nordstrom 1996, 34). Stevenson (2009a) also raises similar issues and alternate viewpoints in the example of grave 133, containing a very large amount of beads. In analysing this grave and attempting to determine the reasons behind the placement of so many beads in this grave, Stevenson (2009a, 187) asserts that in order to understand and fully engage with this mortuary material, the focus should be less on economic dominance and more on 'sociability and spheres of involvement', which would exactly fit with the presence of so much variety of materials and goods to be collected and brought together in the above mentioned graves of these individuals. A crucial point is made by Stevenson (2009a, 187) about the nature of graves with such quantities and varieties of unique objects, which is 'if it had been plundered for its exotic goods, as so many Predynastic burials were, the reliance upon pot counts or grave size would have been rendered the significance of this tomb invisible.' This brings us to the main point of the analysis of these nine graves, as well as to the general reasons for the analyses attempted in this work. The methodology of this study was designed to not to focus on anthropomorphic objects as status or wealth symbols, or on determining whether the graves in which they were placed were wealthy. Instead, the approach was to focus on examining the graves as being constructed and organised by the community and reflecting the life, personhood and significance of the decreased individual, and through this lens to examine the significance and function of these objects.

5.5 SIMILAR OBJECTS IN DIFFERENT GRAVES

Five cases of almost identical-looking objects in two separate graves (a total of 10 graves), all located at Naqada, have been identified in the process of completing the grave catalogue. The individual examples have been discussed in detail in the Chapter 4. The examples in themselves are minimal and considerably more research is needed to discover the possibility of more graves at Naqada sharing identical-looking objects.

What is remarkable in these examples is the objects, especially the two combs (graves 271 and 1757, Figures 45 and 56), the two tags (graves 276 and 1583, Figures 42 and 57) and the El-Ma'mariya figurines and the vessels from Abydos seem to parallel each other, possibly forming one set of objects, which were later split. They seem to form a connection between people buried in two different graves, whether they are related by blood, kinship, community ties or exchanges of reciprocity. Another interesting and plausible possibility is that these objects may have been made by the same person, especially in the case of the two combs and the El-Ma'mariya figurines, which is another indication that ultimately such objects were personal rather than ritualistic or funerary-related items.

5.6 RELATIONSHIP BETWEEN SEX OF THE BODY AND SEX OF THE OBJECT

A significant feature that emerges from the analysis results is the prevalence of female anthropomorphic objects – 60 have been found to be female, with only 19 male objects. Most of the female objects are female figurines, with all tusks and most of the tags not made to look either distinctly male or female. However, using the method described earlier in Chapter 3, some of the tags and combs have been judged to be female, based on several characteristic features strongly suggestive of the female form. These are mainly the hips to waist ratio in the female tags, all of which have the slender 'wasp' waist similar to the Predynastic female figurines. Some of the combs may also be female, on account of the dotted necklaces carved on the anthropomorphic combs' chest areas, which usually only appear on female pin tags. Therefore, the total of all the female objects constitutes more than half of the 118 total objects. The preference for the female image and female form in the use of human imagery in three-dimensional objects is clear.

Intriguingly, this preference is not only found in Predynastic Egypt, but in many other prehistoric civilizations across the world. Any comparisons made between the figurines of these civilizations, however, must be extremely cautions, in order not to mistakenly conclude that a universal trend could exist between cultures separated by distance and time (Knapp and Meskell 1997). Taking this into consideration, Lesure (2002, 595), attempts to uncover why such a pattern exists in many different cultures, and comes to the conclusion that this seemingly universal pattern can be differently explained and assigned meaning to from the unique perspective of each case. Previously proposed theories focus on the values of the female bodies to society in their reproductive capacity as an explanation for the prevalence of female imagery (McNay 1992, 20), while others proposed a universal cult of fertility and motherhood. Lesure (2002, 594) bases his explanations and interpretations of the figurine's meanings in each separate case by closely examining the features and stylistic and design choices made by the makers of the objects and the contexts in which they were used. Using both Near Eastern and Mesoamerican female figurines, he singles out particular details, such as Neolithic Near Eastern female figurines being associated with and deposited in houses. This would explain the choice of the female sex over the male, since women and houses seem to have been two linked concepts (Lesure 2002, 594).

The issue that arises from such a method of analogy is its inability to explain the variety of the figurines, which is predominant among the Predynastic figurines, both male and female. When examining their appearance, one is immediately struck by the diversity in style, pose and the degree of realism and stylisation in each individual example. Several are seated (Figures 28, 29 51 and 59), others are standing, with their elongated lower bodies tapering down into a rounded point (Figures 7, 21, 35, 39 and 60), and in the case of the El-Ma'mariya figurines, each made in an almost exact mould as though part of a collection (Ordynat 2015). The male figurines present just as much variety, therefore in this case it is difficult to determine whether the preference for the female form, so variedly expressed, could be iconographic, social or symbolic in its nature (Lesure 2002, 594). The variety could even be due to some local variation, which is certainly possible when considering the many cemeteries the figurine have been found in. What is clear is that there is certainly a pattern, and it is in some manner related to the funerary rituals and deposition of grave goods at the death of an individual in Predynastic Egyptian culture.

It is equally intriguing, on the other hand, to observe the apparent regularity and stylistic cohesion of the tusks and tags. There is certainly some variation, evident when comparing Figures 40, 42 and 43, all of which come from Naqada but all displaying individuality in their design. However, the size, the rectangular shape and the basic design - with a groove at the bottom for suspension, as well as a pointed face with basic features, and frequent notches and incised decorative lines remain uniform for all anthropomorphic tags. This could be explained by the lack of local variation. As has been mentioned above, almost all anthropomorphic tags come from Naqada, with the exception of five tags from Matmar (Figure 5), look somewhat different to their Naqada counterparts. Tusks all share the same shape due to the nature of their material, which are hippopotamus tusks. All anthropomorphic tusks also have a grooved rounded base and a rounded hollow knot at the top for suspension. The only significant variation comes in either hollowed or solid nature of the tusks – some are hollowed out and left empty, others filled with resin, and still others are left solid. This variability was intentionally created and could be associated with the symbolic meaning of the tusks to their owners.

Anthropomorphic tusks and tags, save only the four who could be identified as possibly female, appear to be deliberately made to avoid looking either male or female, with no identifying sexual characteristics. This is particularly clear in the cases of Figures 30, 43, 44, 62, 63, 68. What they seem to resemble is the general human form, without the necessity to make their sex clear. It has been proposed that the pointed faces of some of the tags may be indicating beards, therefore making most of the tags male (Eyckerman and Hendrickx 2011a). It is possible to discern dashes and notches on some of the faces of the tags and one comb (Figures 34 and 42), but otherwise, defining the sex of the tag by the shape of the face in general is an uncertain and inconclusive method, as it appear to have been unnecessary to contemporaries to have clear indications of sex in the tags' human imagery. It is possible to conclude that the sex of the tag was either irrelevant to the owner and maker, or it was so clear and well understood that there would be no need for overt clarification in the design of the tag. It seems, therefore, that the three dimensional human image in this period was fluid and varied and may have contained a variety of different associations and meanings, depending both on the type of object (figurine, tusk, tag, comb or vessel) and the individual who owned or was associated with the object and was subsequently buried with it.

The available data for analysing the possible associations between the sex of the buried body and the sex and type of the object was quite scarce for figurines, and therefore presented only minor deviations. Anthropomorphic figurines are found in equal numbers in the graves of both men and women. It is not possible to make any stronger conclusions - the distributions appear to be fairly equal between female figurines in women's graves as opposed to male figurines in male graves, and vise-versa. Only five known female graves contained one or more female figurines, and two female graves contained male figurines. Male figurines were found in only three male graves, and only one male grave contained a female figurine. These are small numbers, and it is difficult to perceive any distinct patterns.

In order to get a clearer idea of how such combinations between male and female figurines in burials of both men and women might have been created, a small case study was selected to represent a sample from the cemetery of El-Amrah. This is a rare and peculiar case, in which all known graves with anthropomorphic objects (nine in total) from the cemetery contained only figurines. In addition to this, the sex of the occupant in each grave is known and recorded – these are the separate burials of five men, two women and two children. The real difficulty arises from the methods MacIver and Mace (1903) used to record their excavation. Three of these graves contained figurines the sex of which is impossible to determine, due to the authors not providing photographs, and including minimal descriptions like 'clay doll' (MacIver and Mace 1903, 16). The authors occasionally do classify the figurines as male or female in their descriptions. For example, a figurine from grave B.202 is describes as: 'fragments of clay male doll, with grotesque punch-like head' (MacIver and Mace 1903, 17), with no accompanying photograph. The reasons on which the authors based their conclusion of the figurine being male are unknown and unexplained to us. But in spite of these issues, these graves provide a good example of the versatility of combinations of male and female figurines in graves of men, women and children. Both graves A.57 and A.94 are burials of women, yet the first contained a female figurine and the second a male. One of the two graves containing burials of children also contained a female figurine. In fact, three of the five known child graves in the database contained female figurines, with the other two graves containing fragments of unknown sex. Three male graves at El-Amrah (A.41, A.56 and B.202) contained figurines with identifiable sex, which were all male. Grave A.56 contained two male figurines. What these results show is a variety of combinations, with a possibility of certain preferences. It seems that both sexes could have one or more figurines of either sex deposited in their grave, but there may have been a preference for the sex of the figurine to match the sex of the grave occupant. There is a further possibility that graves of children were usually furnished with female figurines, but this is much less certain, with very little available data.

It is difficult to conclude what these patterns may be telling us about the function of figurines in burials, but it is possible to imagine that in some cases the figurine could have been representing the deceased individual, perhaps having even been made for or by them. As there are almost an equal number of cases in which the sex of the figurine does not match the sex of the body, something different could be suggested. It is certainly not a new notion that prehistoric figurines may be representing actual individuals or ancestral figures from the past, rather than deities or abstract concepts like fertility or protection (Bailey 1994; Lesure 2002; Hamilton 1996), and it is a view that can certainly be applied in this instance. The variety of combinations of both male and female and the lack of any intentional standardisation of style or of placement in the grave suggests that figurines were personal items, perhaps representing real people, and providing memory connections and links between the dead and the living.

The analysis results for placement in male or female graves for tusks and tags are quite different from figurines. The sex of most tusks and tags cannot be identified, therefore only the likelihood of placement in either a male or female grave is under discussion in this section. Most anthropomorphic tusks were found in graves of individuals whose sex could not be determined. Only two graves with known sex of the buried individual contained anthropomorphic tusk pairs – one was a woman's burial, and the other was a multiple burial of six people. Additionally, a female burial in grave 1488 at Naqada, which is included in the database, contained two non-anthropomorphic tusks. It appears that anthropomorphic tags also occur more frequently in the graves of women – 15 graves of women, 4 graves of men and 13 graves of unknown sex contained anthropomorphic tags. Similar results appeared in the study of the Naga ed-Der Cemetery N7000, where tusks and tags occurred very frequently in the graves of women (Podzorski 1993, 124). Eyckerman and Hendrickx (2011a, 521) state that the number of samples is too limited to make a conclusion, and further study into the placement of tusks and tags in the graves of women in Predynastic cemeteries is certainly required to provide a more substantial database. Nevertheless, this statement can be challenged, as there does appear to be a connection between these objects and Predynastic female burials.

When tusks and tags were beginning to be discovered in Predynastic graves, Petrie (1920, 34) proposed that they could be hunting trophies. This suggestion was supported and further developed by Eyckerman and Hendrickx (2011a, 527), who added that tusks and tags were exclusively associated with masculinity. Nowak (2004, 396), noticing the trend of these objects being found in female burials, counter argued that they could not be hunting trophies, being clearly associated with women. However, such conclusions are pre-emptive and would need a variety of social and biological data, not necessarily available to us, to confirm them. In prehistoric societies, the division of labour is generally based on reproductive status (Bentley 1996, 24). Women usually do not engage in hunting because this activity is not compatible with child-bearing, which leads to the assumption that the manufacture of hunting tools and objects that are made from materials obtained through hunting are also exclusively male (Bentley 1996, 24). However, most of the evidence that can be produced in order to inquire into this division of labour and access to materials and crafting in Predynastic society is mortuary, and mortuary context, while having the potential to be misleading and display contradictory patterns, does reflect some version of reality (Costin 1996, 119).

Therefore, the patterns discussed above, although based on a small sample, are nevertheless reoccurring, and should not be ignored. Again, it is difficult to conclude what such patterns could mean, and what function tusks and tags had in the graves of women especially. Yet, it appears that access to hippopotamus ivory and to objects carved and decorated from that material at least were not exclusive to one sex, but appear to be preferred by women. Indeed, the status in the Predynastic graves of women and men, based on the inclusion and exclusion of types of objects or materials in their graves, seems to be equal, perhaps even greater for women (Savage 2000, 93). Women seemed to engage in a greater and more varied number of social roles (Savage 2000, 92), and there is no reason not to accept that some of them may have involved or been associated with tusks and tags.

5.7 MATERIALS

The function and meaning of anthropomorphic objects is closely tied to the materials they are made from, and in the case of figurines especially, there is definitely a preferred material, which is clay.

Clay, both baked and unbaked, is the chosen material for 76% of figurines (37 female figurines, 10 male figurines and 18 fragments). Ivory is the second most common, with 14% of figurines (six female, two male and four fragments), and last is vegetable paste, with 10% of figurines (six female, one male and two fragments).

Anthropomorphic tusks are all made from genuine hippopotamus tusk ivory, but anthropomorphic tags are much more diverse in terms of materials – the majority are made from ivory or bone, but some are made from various types of stone. In addition most of the carved tasks and tags, and some ivory figurines, are incised with black paste, a substance which is used in all tusks and tags but which has not been analysed yet (Eyckerman and Hendrickx 2011a, 508).

Clay is certainly the preferred material for anthropomorphic objects, which is partially explained by the fact that clay is one of the most readily available materials. The most readily available type of clay in Predynastic Egypt would have been Nile silt clay, deposited by the Nile river, which is rich in silica and iron, and turns red to or brown when fired (Bourriau, Nicholson and Rose 2000, 121). Silt clays in general would have been widely available, and local workshops would have existed on a small scale, where clay would have been brought, stored and fired in kilns (Nicholson and Shaw 2000, 122). The choice was also made whether or not to fire the figurine, once it was moulded, since many figurines are unfired, and others are fired to varying degrees (Payne 1993, 16-17). Additionally, clay, unlike carving materials such as stone, bone or ivory, is an extremely malleable when it comes to actually modelling the figurine, and gives the artist the possibility of shaping the arms especially into more imaginative shapes. Ucko (1968, 200) draws attention to the fact that figurines with more complex body postures are usually made of clay.

An interesting feature worth mentioning here is the fact that 65% of figurines were originally painted. In fact, it may have been more than 65%, since it is very difficult to determine whether any of the smaller fragments were painted. Most figurines have a red haematite coating on the surface (Payne 1993, 17), and most of them were also originally painted either in a variety of geometric designs, or in a full coat of red and white, as in the case of the El-Ma'mariya figurines. Therefore, it is safe to say that clay figurines, both female and male, looked very different to their current appearance, with the maker expending effort to apply the geometric patterns all over the figurine, which may have had a symbolic or ritual meaning.

Ivory, while occasionally chosen for the production of human figurines, seems to have been the more popular and established choice for tusks, tags and combs. The Nile was the natural riverine habitat for hippopotamuses, which were known to have been hunted in Ancient Egypt for pest control, for their ivory tusks, and for sport (Krzyszkowska and Morkot 2000, 326). Hippopotamus tusks, therefore, were extensively used to produce a whole variety of objects in the Predynastic, including combs, bracelets, pendants, vessels and pins. The hippopotamus tusks would have been highly prized, both as a material and possibly as a hunting trophy. In fact, when considering how dangerous hippopotamus hunting would have been and how much destruction these animals could cause in cultivated fields, keeping hippopotamus tusks as hunting trophies does not seem unreasonable (Eyckerman and Hendrickx 2011a, 530). It is completely plausible to suggest that part of the meaning for the anthropomorphic carved tusks is related to the hunting of the hippopotamus itself; however, it is questionable whether this implication can be further extended to include the elements of elitism and higher status, as well masculine exclusivity (Eyckerman and Hendrickx 2011a, 530), especially as their funerary context suggests otherwise.

Vegetable paste, when compared to the extent of use of other mentioned materials, is used in a very minor capacity to make figurines. Vegetable paste seems to consist of a concoction of plant remains, which is usually modelled over a reed stick. Vegetable paste was used to model both male and female figurines. Ucko (1968, 186) noticed and commented on this fact, contrary to recent theories about specific materials like vegetable paste being assigned only to female figurines (Eyckerman and Hendrickx 2011b, 533). There is no evidence for any of the before mentioned materials being preferred for either male or female figurines, as can be seen in the results in Chapter 4. A possible reason for the occurrence of more female figurines in vegetable paste is the fact that female figurines were generally preferred and made more frequently than male figurines; hence there are more Predynastic female figurines than male. What is certain is that clay was the most versatile and the most highly used material in the making of anthropomorphic objects. And unlike ivory or stone, the carving of which would require effort to procure the material and some skill to carve, clay was readily available and could have been used by any individual to model their own figurine, even without having access to a kiln. Lastly, Ucko (1968, 427) has previously noted that some 'figurines are…made of durable (and costly) materials, while most of the other figurines are made of more fragile (and cheaper) materials'. Evidently, this choice of material played a role in the figurines' function, depending on its fragility (Ucko 1968, 427).

5.8 OBJECT BREAKAGE

It is clear, from the results of the analysis, that the main group of objects affected by breakage (whether deliberate or not) is female figurines. This could be partially due to the fact that female figurines form the largest part of all anthropomorphic objects from the Predynastic. Only ten of all the recorded female figurines are intact, the rest are broken or fragmented. There are 16 'orphaned' fragments of figurines, which is to say that there were no remains of the rest of the figurine found in the grave. This excludes grave 186 at El-Ma'mariya, in which most of the 21 figurines and fragments are 'orphaned', with parts missing. There are also two examples of tags being broken – the tag from grave 3075 at Matmar has the top half broken off, and the tag from grave 1583 at Naqada appears to have been deliberately cut vertically in half.

Deliberate breakage of objects can be indicated by orphan fragments in closed contexts. These are usually burials, as they suffer little or no later intervention, which allows them to stay looking the way they were originally arranged (Chapman and Gaydarska 2009, 132). The general reasons of breakage can be narrowed down to either accident, split breakage from distribution and reuse, ritual killing or dispersion to ensure fertility or protection (Chapman and Gaydarska 2007, 3). Just like people, some objects underwent 'ritual killing', when they would be 'sacrificed' or broken, specifically for burial (Grinsell 1961, 475). Objects, just like people, often receive the same treatment in the passage of rights rituals such as death, meaning they also 'die' (Ellen, 1988). Other reasons include releasing the spirit contained in the object to accompany the dead and also deliberate destruction of funerary objects in order to prevent them from being used again (Grinsell 1961, 476). In most cases of deliberate breakage, it is pottery that is broken. The deliberate breakage of pottery in Africa is known to be symbolically associated with death, and the making of pottery with life (Barley 1994, 92). In the case of Predynastic Egypt, there are known cases of flint tools and mace heads being broken on purpose (Grinsell 1961, 481). Another more meaningful interpretation is concerned with enchainment and personhood, where the fragments from the same object form a link between the living and the deceased, and where the personal items of the dead were broken and the fragments were distributed between the living and the dead (Chapman and Gaydarska 2009, 132).

The theory of deliberate breakage, especially in terms of human figurines, has been criticised extensively. Generally, criticism of the theory centres along the issues with the lack of evidence for deliberate breakage, and the fact that it is almost always impossible to determine whether the breakage was deliberate. Firstly, it is often argued that the pressure of the soil on figurines from grave contexts makes it entirely plausible that breakages may be due to natural processes. Marangou (1996, 146) when examining Aegean figurines, notes that the breakages are usually along the fragile points of figurines, especially in the joints between the separately moulded parts. Bailey (2001; quoted in Chapman and Gaydarska 2007, 7) asks 'Where is the mundane?', by which he is asserting that if deliberate fragmentation was part of ritualistic behaviour of the community, it would also be evident in the more mundane everyday activities. However, such an assertion is not entirely justified, since deliberate breakage of a personal and possibly valuable possession, especially if it belonged to a deceased loved one, could not be considered in any way a mundane and everyday activity.

Chapman and Gaydarska (2007) conducted an extensive study in which they outlined some possible methods of determining deliberate breakage. The numbers of figurine fragments that are incomplete, when thoroughly analysed by Chapman and Gaydarska, are found to constitute approximately two thirds of all figurines analysed by them from funerary contexts. Over 40% of figurines Chapman and Gaydarska analysed are fragments of either a torso or legs, and only 35% of the figurines are intact.

In the case of the figurines discussed in this study, 80% of the figurines are broken or fragmented. Additionally, as has been stated before, it is evident that the elongated lower limbs of some of the figurines were broken up into several pieces, and in one grave, only one piece broken in such a way has remained (see Figures 100 and 101). Is it possible that these and other Predynastic figurines and tags were broken deliberately? There is evidence to support both a positive and a negative answer to this question. There are documented examples of figurines found broken in pieces and scattered. In the case the Badarian grave 494 at Mostagedda, a female figurine was broken and scattered around the head of the body (Brunton 1937, 89). At the settlement at El-Mahasna, fragments of female figurines were scattered around the areas considered to be of ritual significance (Anderson 2006, 102). In addition, there seems to be a pattern of breakages in female figurines, where the remaining fragment is head and torso, or fragments of the long tapering legs, which seem to have been systematically broken. Lastly, the tag in grave 1583 (Figure 57), is clearly cut in half very cleanly and deliberately.

On the other hand, disintegration of natural material may have taken place in the graves, through which some fragments of figurines may have been completely disintegrated, or had become so unrecognisable as figurine fragments that excavators in the early 20th century would not have recognised them for what they were. This process may have taken place in grave 186 at El-Ma'mariya, where most of the figurine fragments are lower body halves in very poor states of preservation. It is possible that the missing upper parts of the figurines, therefore, disintegrated due to the disturbed and poorly preserved condition of the grave. Some of the breakages seem to indeed be located at the fragile joints – for example, at the joint between the head and the upper body, and the arms. These may have taken place during the plundering on the grave in the past. Yet small fragments of figurine hands and arms survived (Figures 89 to 94) which could indicate deliberate breakage. And furthermore, some graves seems to have multiple intact figurines deposited in them – for example, grave B83 at Abadiya has two intact figurines, grave A.56 at El-Amrah had two intact figurines, and B109 at Abadiya had one intact figurine.

In conclusion, the variety of placement, style and design of the figurines in Predynastic Egypt is an indication of both regional variation and diversity of funerary ritual customs. Therefore, this could extend to include the diversity of deposition – figurines and tags could be placed in the grave whole or broken up, depending on the particular meaning that is placed on the figurine at that particular time in that particular community, and in relation to that specific individual.

CHAPTER 5: DISCUSSION

5.9 THEORIES ON FUNCTION

The aim of this project was to determine the possible function of Predynastic figurines, tusks, tags and combs by analysing the context they come from and the practical aspects of their production. The goal was to steer away from iconographic and stylistic interpretations, and to focus on the practical and to engage in the broader framework of material culture and funerary archaeological theory. Ethnographic examples, based on observation of the use of objects by people in similar environmental and social conditions are extremely helpful when interpreting small human or anthropomorphic figurines, and have been previously used in many defining scholarly works about human figurines (Lesure 2011; Ucko 1962, 1968; Talalay 1993; Voigt 1983, 2000). A further discussion of ethnographic parallels and examples will follow, in order to add to the depth and understanding of the significance of human three-dimensional imagery.

In terms of use and accessibility of materials, and clay especially, it is well known that in past and contemporary documented African societies women dominated pottery and ceramic production (Berns 1993, 130). In having the primary access to and control of clay and production facilities, women were the creators and perpetrators of symbolic and iconographic imagery, constructing meanings for the figurines they made (Berns 1993, 141). Allowing for the possibility that women may have had a general monopoly over the production of clay goods, including pottery and figurines, in the Predynastic may provide an interesting new perspective, and an explanation for the fact that such a majority of Predynastic human figurines were female. It also adds to our perception of how these objects were created and imbued with meaning – understanding material culture and its production involves looking into social strategies and gender dynamics, and allowing for the importance of such dynamics in the function of figurines in the community (Berns 1993, 145).

Additional ethnographic examples of the use and functionality of human imagery could strongly aid the understanding of the possible functions of Predynastic anthropomorphic objects, both realistic and stylised. In general, a figure or icon in itself has great significance, as a link in a chain extending from the maker's mental image, to the viewer (Vansina 1984, 102). The whole process of creating human imagery is shared by the community and communal understanding and indirect or direct involvement – in this sense, works of art or artistic and aesthetic figurative creations are collective and cultural products first and foremost (Vansina 1984, 102). In African communities in general, figurines seem to usually represent real people, rather than deities or abstract concepts. The Yungur people spiritually immortalise their community leaders in clay figurine from, which are then used, either broken or whole, in divination rituals to select new candidates for the positions of chief in the future (Berns 1990, 59). The figurines or fragments of figurines which were once representations of ancestors now serve as the representation of their descendants and successors (Berns 1990, 60). Ancestor figurines of the communities in Northern Kongo are especially made to prevent curses and disease, and therefore serve a protective function for their descendants (Simon and MacGaffey 1995, 49). People from the Luba communities craft special ivory pendants, somewhat reminiscent of Predynastic tags, which are made in the memory of certain revered ancestors (Roberts et. a. 1996, 108). The pendants are suspended from cords along with other objects such as horns, beads and other amulets, and worn either diagonally across the chest or across the arms (Roberts et. al. 1996, 108).

In terms of social context, the question that needs to be asked is: what was the image or object used for? All of these objects come from graves, yet it is evident, especially in the case of tusks and tags, that they were not made specifically for the burial or served solely a funerary function. Figurines are distinct on the basis of their diversity, therefore it is reasonable to assume that their function was varied and ever-changing in day to day practical and spiritual life of Predynastic society. Yet they did serve a function in burials – this is evident from their careful and deliberate placement.

The function of figurines, based on the conducted analysis of their context in this study, has been argued to be personal and emotional – either as a personal possession or self-made object, a rites of passage memorabilia, or a representation of a persona or individual in various social rituals. Tusks, on the other hand, seem to have been owned as an object of prestige, personal display or even memorabilia. They seem to have been conveying a certain message in the social sphere. They could also have had a practical purpose, since some have been hollowed out and filled with resin. It is difficult to determine the exact meaning of such an object, but the deposition of tusks seems to show that they were collected in groups, and valued for their material. They rarely have a connection to the anthropomorphic aspect, since they were so rarely carved in the human image; therefore it is reasonable to assume that their primary function had little to do with the human image symbolism. Tags present a more iconographically structured subject matter, and have several ethnographic parallels. The most reasonable interpretation for the function of tags is as ancestor

representations, with possible protective, medicinal or ritual significance – they still represent people, although in a more abstract style. The grooves and perforations on the bottom of tags are indicative of functionality – whether they were worn or tied onto the body with leather straps, it seems clear that they were objects of adornment, and their function was linked with them being physically close to the body, and possibly in pairs or groups.

Lastly, attention should be brought to the nearly identical parallel examples of objects from two different graves, and to the possibility of deliberate breakage. There are several clear examples of objects being deliberately split, or placed in separate graves. What this shows is that anthropomorphic objects were first and foremost the personal possessions of individuals, individuals with emotions, memories and deep social and kinship connections. What can be seen and expressed though the placement of objects in Predynastic graves are these connections and links, which appears to be the most important general function of these objects. They played a crucial role in the formation of personhood and individuality, social roles and connections and collective community identity. They need to be perceived and examined firstly as items of personal significance, rather than iconographic and symbolic pieces of Predynastic art. When viewed in this alternative light, their practical every day functions are placed in the background, in terms of greater understanding on Predynastic people and society. What emerges is the importance of these objects in representing imagery that was significant to individuals on a personal level, whether it was to preserve a memory, receive protection or blessing from ancestors, or to form part of a ritual.

CHAPTER 6: CONCLUSION

This study began by asking the question of whether it is possible to identify the function of Predynastic anthropomorphic three-dimensional objects from examining their context in Predynastic graves. The results produced by this work are complex and multilayered, and reflect the distinct diversity of the objects themselves, in both their outward appearance and their particular placements in graves. The results allow us to confirm that it is indeed possible to observe the functions of anthropomorphic objects through their context. On the basis of the placements of figurines it is possible to conclude that they were used largely as personal and emotional items by both the deceased individuals and their friends and relations. They seem to have been functioning as representations of individuals or even the deceased themselves, which is reflected in their individual styles and design – representations which were familiar and recognised by the people who placed them in the grave. On the other hand, tusks, tags and combs, usually forming part of a larger collection of ivory objects in graves, and having equivalent non-anthropomorphic counterparts, function as less personal and more complementary burial objects. Tusks, tags and combs seem to have had a primary function which was not associated specifically with anthropomorphic imagery, and which developed to include it into the objects' appearance.

The anthropomorphic element seems to have has a much more significant and prominent meaning in the case of the figurines, while being, as stated above, seemingly secondary to that of tusks, tags and combs. The full function of the figurines appears to be centred on the human image and its versatility and individuality, which certainly reflects the more personal connection evident from their careful and close placements to the body in the grave. Additionally, figurines, more than any other type of object, are found broken up, or fragmented in the grave, which could be a sign of deliberate breakage of a personal object, with pieces distributed for the sake of memory. The central focus of the meaning of tusks, however, seems to be first and foremost on the material from which they are made. This also applies to a lesser extend to tags and combs. Tags certainly possess a strong and distinctive element of anthropomorphic imagery, yet this element is also more abstract in both their design and in their placement. They seems to represent collections rather than individual personal items, and their placement (laid out along the arm, or tied together with leather straps) is more indicative of the function they may have served in life, as magical or protective items. Similarly, combs also form part of collections in graves, and the appearance anthropomorphic imagery is rare and likely decorative in their case.

It terms of the status of the burials with anthropomorphic objects, the research established that there is no clear association between these objects and luxury or rare items, and that they are not found solely in wealthy graves. This seems to indicate that anthropomorphic objects had no association to elite social status, power or authority. In fact, the diversity of object collections in the graves where anthropomorphic objects were found may signify that the individuals buried with them may have held specific social roles and played a particular part in the community life. What is clear about the context of these objects is the fact that they were placed very deliberately and carefully, and this was clearly important to the individuals who arranged the burial. Moreover, as the several cases of identical objects in different graves shows, objects linked people to each other, which is another clear indication that their context was significant and did in fact reflect their in Predynastic society and burial practices.

The data collected here has already been partially examined in large all-encompassing works by Ucko (1968), Baumgartel (1960) and Eyckerman and Hendrickx (2011a), as well as smaller studies focussing specifically on one type of object (Nowak 2004, Brovarski 2005). The uniqueness of this study, however, consists in viewing the data not from an iconographic and all-encompassing perspective, but from the contextual one, with the inclusion of material culture and mortuary archaeology theory in its methodological approach. The study conducted in this work, while drawing on previous work of Predynastic scholars, also utilised the new potential of the ideas proposed by Stevenson (2009a, 2013). It focused on further testing Stevenson's new methodological approaches to Predynastic mortuary data, especially in regards to burial aesthetics and social relationships reflected in burial goods and arrangements, and applying them to the collected data in order to obtain much more information and understanding of the Predynastic burial practices. In combining these elements and in focusing particularly on the context, this study in quite unique and significant in its approach, and produces results that have not been considered or discussed before in previous studies of Predynastic anthropomorphic objects.

Naturally, many limitations to the analysis and the data itself prevented a deeper and lengthier study from being conducted. In this small, highly in-depth study, the data had to be confined to a specific time period and to specific types of objects, in order scale down an analysis that could become all-encompassing, in order to fit the parameters within which the research was carried out. Many additional objects from earlier and later periods, as well as Predynastic depictions of the human image manifested in a variety of forms could have been included to enhance and enrich our understanding of anthropomorphic imagery and its meaning. Additionally, the study avoided any further in-depth iconographic analysis, which in itself would greatly enhance the scope and the resulting interpretations arrived at in the discussion of this study. It is important to stress that the study of anthropomorphic three-dimensional imagery has been artificially isolated for the purposes of this work, but it is essentially part of a much larger body of data and warrants future investigation.

The study of anthropomorphic three-dimensional imagery forms part of a larger enquiry into the emergence of human imagery and human depiction and its development and growth through the Predynastic and into the Dynastic period. The human figure is represented in an abundance if ways and styles in Predynastic art. Perhaps the most iconic, apart from human figurines, are the painted vases, commonly knows and C-Ware and D-Ware. The imagery depicted on these vessels is of a variety of figures, both male and female, often interpreted as dancing or fighting (Garfinkel 2003). The famous examples of C-Ware from Abydos seem to depict figures entwined together, often with their arms raised in a similar pose to the El-Ma'mariya figurines (Eyckerman and Hendrickx 2012, 26-27). These images are often interpreted as showing power or dominance, which may have later evolved into the standard Egyptian Dynastic royal iconography. The imagery from D-Ware vessels centres more frequently on figures lined up on boats and interacting with the natural and animal world (Patch 2011, 70-75). The figures with upraised arms also appear frequently and are always depicted in the centre of the composition. Other rarer examples of human depiction include tomb painting, as is the case of The Painted Tomb (Tomb 100) at Hierakonpolis. The Painted Tomb is full of images of humans interacting with animals, and is frequently argued to be depicting humans exerting power over and attempting to control the natural world. This interpretation seems to have some archaeological evidence to prove it, as the cemetery of Hierakonpolis is abundant with animal burials (Friedman 2011, 88). Later examples of human imagery, dating to the Naqada III period, include a large number of decorative palettes. The most prominent examples include the Two Dog Palette, The Hunters Palette and the Battlefield Palette, all of which date to Naqada III (Patch 2011, 137-140). The theme of dominance and conflict is very evident in these examples, the styles of which are visibly different from the human depictions found in the tusks, tags and figurines previously discussed. What is evident is the progress and the changing nature of the thematic and stylistic trends of Predynastic art from the very beginning, and that future research in the area of Predynastic iconography, and human imagery in particular, would indeed benefit from studies that would examine the emergence of human depiction in Egypt and follow its development from the Predynastic into the early Dynastic times.

CHAPTER 6: CONCLUSION

The research conducted in this study has generated many additional questions that could be answered by future studies on the subject. Firstly, an investigation into the context of resin and malachite could be conducted in order to discern what their typical placement in Predynastic grave was and what function these materials may have had in their mortuary contexts and well as in daily life. Secondly, a detailed analysis of the burial contexts of all known tusks and tags could provide some noteworthy insight into their function and importance in burials, and their meaning as objects of daily use. Thirdly, a juxtaposition of the settlement and mortuary data, both in terms of figurines and in general terms of material and objects use could provide us with a much better understanding of the relationship between the living and the dead in Predynastic society. Similar studies on other archaeological contexts have been done in the past, and a study of the same scope, based especially on the use of material culture and iconography in burials in contrast to everyday life could give us insight into the meaning and significance of tusks, tags and figurines in Predynastic burials. In general, further research into the arrangement of Predynastic burials would be of particular importance in providing us with a clearer picture of the relationship of the Predynastic community with material culture, and its social and ritual significance.

APPENDIX I: THE OBJECT CATALOGUE

	TYPE	DATE	LOCATION	TOMB	MATERIAL	SEX	CONDITION	TOMB POSITION	SEX OF BODIES	TOMB CONDITION	ACCOCIATED OBJECTS	
1	Tusk	S.D. 37 - 38	El-Badari	Tomb 3165	Ivory, incised	Type 1; M	Broken	In container; with objects	U	U, Intact?	Pot; tusks; tags	1
2	Figurine	S.D. 38 - 44	El-Badari	Tomb 3740	Veg. Paste; on reed	F	Unknown	In container; found on body	M; F	Intact	Basket; resin	2
3	Tusk	S.D. 44	El-Badari	Tomb 3828	Ivory, incised	Type 2; U	Broken; fragments		U	Plundered	Resin?	3
4	Fragment	S.D. 49 - 53	Qau	Tomb 113	Clay; painted red, black, white	U	Broken; head only	U	U	U	U	4
5	Tag	S.D. 37 - 57	Matmar	Tomb 2682	Ivory, incised	F	Intact	In container; tied by leather	M	U	Wooden box; tags	5
6	Tag	S.D. 37 - 57	Matmar	Tomb 2682	Ivory, incised	F	Intact	In container; tied by leather	M	U	Wooden box; tags	6
7	Tag	S.D. 37 - 57	Matmar	Tomb 2682	Ivory, incised	F	Intact	In container; tied by leather	M	U	Wooden box; tags	7
8	Tag	S.D. 37 - 57	Matmar	Tomb 2682	Ivory, incised	F	Intact	In container; tied by leather	M	U	Wooden box; tags	8
9	Tag	S.D. 38	Matmar	Tomb 3075	Ivory, incised	U	Broken; body only	U	U	U	U	9
10	Fragment	S.D. 39?	Matmar	Tomb 2643	Veg. paste on reed; painted red	U	Broken; fragments	U	M	U	Resin?	10
11	Figurine	S.D. 39?	Mostagedda	Tomb 1832	Ivory, incised	F	Intact	At hands; with objects	U	Intact	Resin; palette	11

12	Figurine	S.D. 39?	Mostagedda	Tomb 1872	Limestone	F	Broken; body only	U	C	Disturbed	U	12
13	Fragment	S.D. 51	El-Mahasna	Tomb H.33	Clay; painted red	U	Broken; body only	At skull	U	Plundered	U	13
14	Fragment	S.D. 42	El-Mahasna	Tomb H.42	Clay	U	Broken; fragments	South end of grave	M; U; U	Intact	U	14
15	Fragment	S.D. 41	El-Mahasna	Tomb H.97	Clay; painted red	U	Broken; head only	U	U	Plundered	U	15
16	Fragment	S.D. 60	El-Mahasna	Tomb H.85	Clay; painted red	U	Broken; fragments	U	C	Disturbed	U	16
17	Figurine	S.D. 41	El-Mahasna	Tomb H.29	Ivory	M	Whole	South end of grave	F; U	Intact	Tusks	17
18	Fragment	S.D. 41	El-Mahasna	Tomb H.29	Clay; painted red	U	Broken; fragments	Behind head	F	Intact	U	18
19	Fragment	S.D. 41	El-Mahasna	Tomb H.29	Clay; painted red	U	Broken; fragments	Behind head	F	Intact	U	19
20	Figurine	S.D. 56	El-Mahasna	Tomb H.41	Veg. Paste	F	Whole	Found on body	F	Plundered	Mace head	20
21	Figurine	S.D. 41	El-Amrah	Tomb A.41	Clay	M	U	U	M	Plundered	U	21
22	Fragment	S.D. 41	El-Amrah	Tomb A.57	Clay	F	Broken; fragments	In container	F	Plundered	Basket	22
23	Figurine	S.D. 41	El-Amrah	Tomb A.72	Clay	U	U	U	M	Plundered	U	23
24	Figurine	S.D. 41	El-Amrah	Tomb A.74	Clay; painted red	F	U	In container?	C	U	Basket?	24

APPENDIX I: THE OBJECT CATALOGUE

25	Fragment	S.D. 41	El-Amrah	Tomb A.117	Clay	U	Broken; head only	U	C	U	Malachite?	25
26	Fragment	S.D. 41	El-Amrah	Tomb A.90	Clay	U	Broken; head only	U	M	U	U	26
27	Figurine	S.D. 46	El-Amrah	Tomb A.56	Clay; painted red	M	Whole	U	M	Plundered	U	27
28	Figurine	S.D. 46	El-Amrah	Tomb A.56	Clay; painted red	M	Whole	U	M	Plundered	U	28
29	Figurine	S.D. 41	El-Amrah	Tomb A.94	Veg. Paste, painted red	M	Whole	U	F	Plundered	U	29
30	Fragment	S.D. 41	El-Amrah	Tomb B.202	Clay	M	Broken; head only	In container?	M	Plundered	Basket?	30
31	Figurine	S.D. 33 – 48	Abadiya	Tomb B83	Clay; painted red	M	Broken; body only	U	U	Plundered	U	31
32	Figurine	S.D. 33 – 48	Abadiya	Tomb B83	Clay; painted red	M	Broken; body only	U	U	Plundered	U	32
33	Figurine	S.D. 33 – 48	Abadiya	Tomb B83	Clay; painted red	F	Whole	U	U	Plundered	U	33
34	Figurine	S.D. 33 – 48	Abadiya	Tomb B83	Clay; painted red	F	Whole	U	U	Plundered	U	34
35	Figurine	S.D. 33 – 48	Abadiya	Tomb B83	Clay; painted red	M	Whole	U	U	Plundered	U	35
36	Figurine	S.D. 33 – 48	Abadiya	Tomb B83	Clay; painted red	M	Whole	U	U	Plundered	U	36
37	Figurine	S.D. 34 – 41	Abadiya	Tomb B101	Clay on reed; painted black	F	Broken; body only	North end of grave	U	Plundered	U	37

38	Figurine	S.D. 34 - 41	Abadiya	Tomb B101	Clay on reed; painted white	F	Broken; body only	North end of grave	U	Plundered	U	38
39	Figurine	S.D. 34 - 41	Abadiya	Tomb B101	Clay on reed; painted black	F	Broken; body only	North end of grave	U	Plundered	U	39
40	Fragment	S.D. 34 - 41	Abadiya	Tomb B101	Clay on reed	U	Broken; body only	North end of grave	U	Plundered	U	40
41	Fragment	S.D. 34 - 41	Abadiya	Tomb B101	Clay	U	Broken; head only	North end of grave	U	Plundered	U	41
42	Fragment	S.D. 34 - 41	Abadiya	Tomb B101	Clay on reed	U	Broken; head only	North end of grave	U	Plundered	U	42
49	Tag	Naqada IIb?	Naqada	Tomb T4	Slate	U	Whole	South end of grave; tied by leather	M; M; M; F; U; U	Disturbed	Tusks, tags, ostrich egg shell	49
50	Tag	Naqada IIb?	Naqada	Tomb T4	Slate	U	Whole	South end of grave; tied by leather	M; M; M; F; U; U	Disturbed	Tusks, tags, ostrich egg shell	50
51	Tusk	Naqada IIb?	Naqada	Tomb T4	Ivory; incised	Type 2; U	Whole	South end of grave	M; M; M; F; U; U	Disturbed	Tusks, tags, ostrich egg shell	51
52	Tag	Naqada II?	Naqada	Tomb T24	Ivory; incised	U	Whole	U	U	U	Tags	52
53	Tusk	Naqada IIb?	Naqada	Tomb 226	Ivory; incised	Type 2; U	Whole	U	U	U	Tusks	53
54	Comb	Naqada IIb?	Naqada	Tomb 268	Ivory	M	Broken	In front of body; in container; with objects	U	U	Pot; tag	54
55	Figurine	Naqada IIa?	Naqada	Tomb 271	Ivory; incised	F	Whole	Behind body; east end of grave; in a row	U	Plundered	Figurines	55

APPENDIX I: THE OBJECT CATALOGUE

56	Figurine	Naqada IIa?	Naqada	Tomb 271	Ivory; incised	F	Broken; body only	Behind body; east end of grave; in a row	U	Plundered	Figurines
57	Figurine	Naqada IIa?	Naqada	Tomb 271	Ivory; incised	F	Broken; body only	Behind body; east end of grave; in a row	U	Plundered	Figurines
58	Fragment	Naqada IIa?	Naqada	Tomb 271	Ivory; incised	F	Broken; head only	Behind body; east end of grave; in a row	U	Plundered	Figurines
59	Figurine	Naqada IIa?	Naqada	Tomb 271	Veg. paste on reed; painted black	F	Whole	North end of grave	U	Plundered	U
60	Tag	Naqada IIa?	Naqada	Tomb 271	Slate; shell	U	Whole	In container; with objects	U	Plundered	Basket; tusks; malachite; resin
61	Fragment	S.D. 32 - 48	Naqada	Tomb 273	Ivory	U	Broken; fragments	U	U	U	U
62	Tag	Naqada IIb?	Naqada	Tomb 276	Ivory	U	Whole	U	U	U	U
63	Tag	Naqada IIb?	Naqada	Tomb 276	Ivory	U	Whole	U	U	U	U
64	Tag	Naqada IIb?	Naqada	Tomb 276	Ivory	U	Whole	U	U	U	U
65	Tag	Naqada IIa?	Naqada	Tomb 1329	Ivory	U	Whole	U	F	U	U
66	Tag	Naqada IIa?	Naqada	Tomb 1329	Alabaster	U	Whole	U	F	U	U
67	Comb	Naqada IIb?	Naqada	Tomb 1411	Ivory	U	Broken	U	U	U	U
68	Fragment	S.D. 35 - 68	Naqada	Tomb 1413	Veg. Paste, painted red; black	F	Broken; body only	U	U	U	U

EGYPTIAN PREDYNASTIC ANTHROPOMORPHIC OBJECTS

69	Fragment	S.D. 35 - 68	Naqada	Tomb 1413	Veg. Paste, painted red	F	Broken; body only	U	U	U	U
70	Tusk	Naqada IIa?	Naqada	Tomb 1419	Ivory; incised	U	Whole	In front of body; tied by leather	F	U	Tusks
71	Tusk	Naqada IIa?	Naqada	Tomb 1419	Ivory; incised	U	Whole	In front of body; tied by leather	F	U	Tusks
72	Figurine	Naqada IIa?	Naqada	Tomb 1488	Clay	F	Broken	Behind head	F	U	Mace head
73	Figurine	Naqada IIa?	Naqada	Tomb 1488	Clay; on reed	F	Broken	Behind head	F	U	Mace head
74	Fragment	Naqada IIa?	Naqada	Tomb 1503	Clay;; painted black	U	Broken; body only	U	U	U	U
75	Figurine	Naqada IIa?	Naqada	Tomb 1530	Clay;; painted black; red	F	Broken; body only	U	U	U	U
76	Fragment	Naqada IIa?	Naqada	Tomb 1530	Clay; on reed; painted red	U	Broken; fragments	U	U	U	U
77	Fragment	Naqada IIa?	Naqada	Tomb 1546	Clay;; painted black; red	U	Broken; wig only	U	M	U	U
78	Fragment	Naqada IIa?	Naqada	Tomb 1546	Clay;; painted black; red	U	Broken; wig only	U	M	U	U
79	Comb	Naqada IIa?	Naqada	Tomb 1561	Ivory	U	Broken	U	U	U	U
80	Tag	Naqada IIb?	Naqada	Tomb 1583	Ivory	U	Half	Between bodies	U; U	U	Tusks; tags; resin
81	Figurine	Naqada IIa?	Naqada	Tomb 1611	Clay; painted red	F	Broken	U	U	U	U

APPENDIX I: THE OBJECT CATALOGUE

82	Figurine	Naqada IIa?	Naqada	Tomb 1687	Clay;; painted black	F	Broken; body only	U	U	U	U	82
83	Figurine	Naqada IIa?	Naqada	Tomb 1677	Ivory	F	Broken	U	U	U	U	83
84	Fragment	Naqada IIa?	Naqada	Tomb 1705	Veg. Paste	U	Broken; fragments	U	U	U	U	84
85	Tag	Naqada IIa?	Naqada	Tomb 1757	Siltstone	U	Whole	U	U	U	U	85
86	Tag	Naqada IIa?	Naqada	Tomb 1757	Siltstone	U	Whole	U	U	U	U	86
87	Tag	Naqada IIa?	Naqada	Tomb 1757	Ivory	U	Whole	U	U	U	U	87
88	Fragment	Naqada IIa?	Naqada	Tomb 1788	Clay; painted black; red	U	Broken; wig only	U	C	U	U	88
89	Figurine	Naqada IIa-b	Hierakonpolis	Tomb 72	Ivory	M	Whole	In container; with objects; west end of grave	U	Intact	Vessel; wooden box/basket	89
90	Figurine	Naqada IIa-b	Hierakonpolis	Tomb 72	Clay	F	Broken; body only	U	U	Intact	U	90
91	Tag	Naqada IIa-b	Hierakonpolis	Tomb B33	Stone	U	Whole	In container; with objects; in front of body	F	Intact	Stone pendants; red ore; galena; pebbles; bone tools; comb; lithics; shell; resin; plant remains; clay; wood	91
92	Figurine	S.D 33-34	Abydos	Tomb U21	Clay; painted red	F	Broken; fragments	U	U	Plundered	U	92

67

93	Vessel	Naqada IIa	Abydos	Tomb U502	Clay; painted white	F	Whole	East end of grave	U	Disturbed	U	93
94	Figurine	Naqada IIa	Abydos	Tomb U502	Clay; painted white	M	Broken; body only	U	U	Disturbed	Malachite?	94
95	Figurine	Naqada IIa	Abydos	Tomb U502	Clay; painted white	M	Broken; body only	U	U	Disturbed	Malachite?	95
96	Figurine	Naqada IIa	El-Ma'mariya	Tomb 2	Clay; painted white	F	Whole	At skull	U	U	Resin; Lithics	96
97	Figurine	Naqada IIa	El-Ma'mariya	Tomb 2	Clay; painted white	F	Whole	At skull	U	U	Resin; Lithics	97
98	Figurine	Naqada IIa	El-Ma'mariya	Tomb 186	Clay; painted white	F	Broken	U	U	Disturbed	U	98
99	Figurine	Naqada IIa	El-Ma'mariya	Tomb 186	Clay; painted white	F	Broken	U	U	Disturbed	U	99
100	Figurine	Naqada IIa	El-Ma'mariya	Tomb 186	Clay; painted white	F	Broken	U	U	Disturbed	U	100
101	Figurine	Naqada IIa	El-Ma'mariya	Tomb 186	Clay; painted white	F	Broken	U	U	Disturbed	U	101
102	Figurine	Naqada IIa	El-Ma'mariya	Tomb 186	Clay; painted white	F	Broken	U	U	Disturbed	U	102
103	Figurine	Naqada IIa	El-Ma'mariya	Tomb 186	Clay; painted white	F	Broken	U	U	Disturbed	U	103
104	Figurine	Naqada IIa	El-Ma'mariya	Tomb 186	Clay; painted white	F	Broken; body only	U	U	Disturbed	U	104
105	Figurine	Naqada IIa	El-Ma'mariya	Tomb 186	Clay; painted white	F	Broken; body only	U	U	Disturbed	U	105

APPENDIX I: THE OBJECT CATALOGUE

106	Figurine	Naqada IIa	El-Ma'mariya	Tomb 186	Clay; painted white	F	Broken; body only	U	U	U	Disturbed	U	106
107	Figurine	Naqada IIa	El-Ma'mariya	Tomb 186	Clay; painted white	F	Broken; body only	U	U	U	Disturbed	U	107
108	Figurine	Naqada IIa	El-Ma'mariya	Tomb 186	Clay; painted white	F	Broken; body only	U	U	U	Disturbed	U	108
109	Figurine	Naqada IIa	El-Ma'mariya	Tomb 186	Clay; painted white	F	Broken; body only	U	U	U	Disturbed	U	109
110	Figurine	Naqada IIa	El-Ma'mariya	Tomb 186	Clay; painted white	F	Broken; body only	U	U	U	Disturbed	U	110
111	Figurine	Naqada IIa	El-Ma'mariya	Tomb 186	Clay; painted white	F	Broken; body only	U	U	U	Disturbed	U	111
112	Figurine	Naqada IIa	El-Ma'mariya	Tomb 186	Clay; painted white	F	Broken; body only	U	U	U	Disturbed	U	112
113	Fragment	Naqada IIa	El-Ma'mariya	Tomb 186	Clay	U	Broken; arm only	U	U	U	Disturbed	U	113
114	Fragment	Naqada IIa	El-Ma'mariya	Tomb 186	Clay	U	Broken; arm only	U	U	U	Disturbed	U	114
115	Fragment	Naqada IIa	El-Ma'mariya	Tomb 186	Clay	U	Broken; arm only	U	U	U	Disturbed	U	115
116	Fragment	Naqada IIa	El-Ma'mariya	Tomb 186	Clay	U	Broken; arm only	U	U	U	Disturbed	U	116
117	Fragment	Naqada IIa	El-Ma'mariya	Tomb 186	Clay	U	Broken; arm only	U	U	U	Disturbed	U	117
118	Fragment	Naqada IIa	El-Ma'mariya	Tomb 186	Clay	U	Broken; arm only	U	U	U	Disturbed	U	118

APPENDIX II: ADDITIONAL GRAVES

MATMAR

Grave 2660: Intact grave, female burial, two tags. Tags found near the head, in a basket that also contained malachite, galena, and a single pebble.

Grave 2720: Intact grave, female burial, three tags. Tags found close to the hands, with a palette.

MAHASNA

Grave B75: Intact grave, female burial, three tags. The tags were found laid out along the forearm of the body.

Grave H18: Two tusks, laid on top of a large rhombic palette, were found close to the face of the body.

Grave H45: Two ivory tusks were found near the pelvis of the body. To the south of the tusks were two more tusks.

Grave H61: Female burial. On the left side of the chest lay a tag and a rhombic palette.

NAQADA

Grave 1426: In front of knees were three ivory tusks, one solid and two hollow.

Grave 1586: Male body. Two ivory combs were found behind the head.

MOSTAGEDDA

Grave 320: Ivory combs were found at the hands of the body.

Grave 1632: An ivory comb and tag lay over the body.

Grave 1857: Intact grave, female burial. At the hands were found a rhombic palette, a pebble, a basket containing malachite, two flint flakes, and three limestone tags with traces of leather at the top, for suspension.

Grave 1880: Intact female. At elbows: bones of small animal, rhomboid palette, above which was small basket containing malachite and a wooden comb with ibex, and a string of soapstone beads.

APPENDIX III: ASSOCIATED OBJECTS

	Grave 3165, Badari	Grave 3740, Badari	Grave 1832, Mostagedda	Grave H. 42, Mahasna	Grave H. 41, Mahasna	Grave H. 29, Mahasna	Grave T4, Naqada	Grave 72, HK6	Grave B33, HK 43
Female Figurines	No	1, vegetable paste on stick	1, ivory	No	Yes, clay	No	No	Yes, 1	No
Male Figurines	No	No	No	No	No	Yes, 1 (ivory)	No	Yes, 1 (ivory)	No
Figurine Fragments	No	No	No	Yes	No	Yes, 2 fragments	No	No	No
Anthropomorphic Tusks	1	No	No	No	No	No	Yes, 1	No	No
Anthropomorphic Tags	No	No	No	No	No	No	Yes, 3	No	Yes, 1 (stone)
Plain Tusks	No	No	No	No	No	Yes, 4	Yes, 1	Yes, 3	No
Plain Tags	8 ivory tags (2 pairs, a set of 3 and one small one)	No	No	No	Yes, 1 (ivory)	No	No	No	Yes, 5*
Combs	1 ivory comb, plain	No	No	No	Yes, 1 (ivory)	No	Yes, 1 (bone)	Yes, 10	Yes, 1 (ivory)*
Resin	Yes	Yes, with figurine	Yes	No	Yes (at feet and neck of body)	Yes, also resin beads	No	No	Yes, in leather bag and a large separate chunk
Malachite	Yes	No	No	No	No	Yes (in shells)	No	Yes	No
Black-Topped Pottery	No	Yes, 3 (B25s3, B25b, B62m4)	No	Yes, 7 (B27g, B55b, B26dx5)	Yes, 8 (B26d, B65b, B62d, B26b, B28m, B25j, B52a, B25h)	Yes, 4 (B250, B25p, B25q, B27c)	Yes, 10 (B11f (x2), B35c, B47, B58c, B62a, B72a (x2), B74a, B74b)		Yes, 4 pots
Rough Pottery	No	No	No	No	No	No	Yes, 6 (R81x2, R91a/bx4)	No	No

EGYPTIAN PREDYNASTIC ANTHROPOMORPHIC OBJECTS

	1, T7	P38h		P63a	P11d.				
Red Polished Pottery			No			Yes, 2 (P7a, P4b)	Yes, 5 (P22, P22a, P24l, P56ax2)	Yes, 1 (decorated with lion)	No
C-Ware or D-Ware	No	No	No	No	No	Yes, 1 (C-Ware pot with animal designs)	No	No	No
Fancy Pottery	Ivory bowl	F12	No	No	No	No	F14	No	No
Animal Bones	No	Yes, calf	No	Yes, 2 animals (goat/antelope)	No	Yes (ox)	No	Yes, 2 cows, sheep/goat	Yes, 5 polished tools*
Carnelian	No	Yes, beads	No	No	Yes	Yes, beads	No	No	No
Steatite	No	Yes, glazed beads	No	No	Yes, glazed	Yes, glazed beads	No	No	No
Calcite	Yes, pendant	No	No	No	No	No	No	No	No
Lead Ore	No	No	No	No	No	No	No	No	Yes
Sulphate of Lime	No	No	No	No	No	Yes	No	No	No
Alabaster	Yes, a stud/peg	No	No	No	No	No	Yes, 1 vase	No	No
Limestone	Yes, 2 spindle whorls	Yes, mace head	No	No	No	Yes, vase	Yes, 1 vase	No	No
Shell	Yes, string of 4 Natica, 15 Oliva, 24 Conus	No	No	No	Yes	2 shells	No	No	Yes, 1 (shell pendant)*
Ivory Objects	11 total	No	Yes, 3 (1 bracelet and 2 cowries)	No	3 ivory bracelets, 1 ivory comb	Yes, 11 (5 ivory bracelets, 2 bowls, 2 pins, 2 combs)	No	No	No

APPENDIX II: ADDITIONAL GRAVES

Mace Heads	Yes, granite disk mace-head	Yes, 1	No	No	Yes,1 (diorite)	Yes, 1 (clay)	No	No	No
Palettes	Yes, 2 palettes (one rhombic, one large)	Yes, 1	Yes, 1	No	No	Yes, 2	Yes, 2	Yes, 2 (diorite)	Yes, 1 (greywacke)
Pebbles	Yes, 7 + 24 flint pebbles	Yes, 1	No	No	No	Yes, 2	No	Yes, 8	No
Haematite	No	No	No	No	Yes	Yes, beads	Yes	No	No
Red Ochre	Yes	No	No	No	No	No	No	Yes, found in tusks	Yes
Copper	No	No	No	No	No	No	No	No	No
Silver	No	No	No	No	Yes	No	No	No	No
Gold	No	No	No	No	Yes	No	No	No	No
Ostrich Egg Shells	No	No	No	No	No	No	Yes	No	No
Leather	No	No	No	No	No	No	No	No	Yes, 2 leather bags*
Wood	Yes, fragments	Wood planks for roofing	No	No	No	No	No	No	Yes, fragments*
Clay Objects	No	No	No	Yes, 1 (small clay cup-shaped perforated object)	Yes (3 clay cups, board game, 7 rattling small objects, clay pendant)	No	No	No	Clay cones*, some found in leather bag
Grain/Wheat	Yes	No	No	No	No	No	No	No	No

EGYPTIAN PREDYNASTIC ANTHROPOMORPHIC OBJECTS

Flint Tools/ Flakes	Yes, 3	No	No	No	No	No	No	Yes, 1	Yes, 34	Yes, 3*
Basket	No	Yes, 2	No	No	No	No	No	No	No	Yes, 1 (containing objects marked with *)
Matting	No	No	No	Yes	No	No	No	No	Yes	No
Other Objects	83 nummulities/fossils? (not pierced)	No	No	No	Pierced clay cup, game board & pieces, 'garlic' moulds	Burnt organic matter, mussel shells	No	No	Plant remains*, fabric pillow

APPENDIX IV - LIST OF OBJECTS AND FIGURES

FIGURE 1
Map of Predynastic Sites in Egypt
From K. Bard, 'The Egyptian Predynastic: A Review of the Evidence', (1994), *Journal of Egyptian Archaeology*, 21, 265-288, Figure 1.

OBJECT 1 (FIGURE 2)
Tusk, Grave 3165, El-Badari
From G. Brunton and G. Caton-Thompson, *The Badarian Civilization and the Predynastic Civilization near Badari*, (1928), London: B. Quaritch LTD, Pl. LXX, 16.

OBJECT 2 (FIGURE 3)
Figurine, Grave 3740, El-Badari
Similar type of figurine is found in W. M. F. Petrie, *Prehistoric Egypt*, (1920), Pl. XLV, 29.
From W. M. F. Petrie, *Prehistoric Egypt*, (1920), London: B. Quaritch LTD, Pl. XLV, 29.

OBJECT 3
Tusk, Grave 3828, El-Badari
No image, only description: '...had no loop, but at the pointed end the vestiges of a human head remained in the shape of two eyes and sloping lines, incised in black.', G. Brunton and G.Caton-Thompson, *The Badarian Civilization And the Predynastic Civilization near Badari*, (1928), London: B. Quaritch LTD, 51.

OBJECT 4 (FIGURE 4)
Fragment, Grave 133, Qau
From G. Brunton and G. Caton-Thompson, *The Badarian Civilization and the Predynastic Civilization near Badari*, (1928), London: B. Quaritch LTD, Pl. LXX, 45.

OBJECT 5 (FIGURE 5)
Tags, Grave 2682, Matmar
From G. Brunton, *Matmar*, (1948), London: B. Quaritch LTD, PL. XVII, 29-32.

OBJECT 6 (FIGURE 5)
Tags, Grave 2682, Matmar
From G. Brunton, *Matmar*, (1948), London: B. Quaritch LTD, PL. XVII, 29-32.

OBJECT 7 (FIGURE 5)
Tags, Grave 2682, Matmar
From G. Brunton, *Matmar*, (1948), London: B. Quaritch LTD, PL. XVII, 29-32.

OBJECT 8 (FIGURE 5)
Tags, Grave 2682, Matmar
From G. Brunton, *Matmar*, (1948), London: B. Quaritch LTD, PL. XVII, 29-32.

OBJECT 9 (FIGURE 6)
Tag, Grave 3075, Matmar
From G. Brunton, *Matmar*, (1948), London: B. Quaritch LTD, PL. XVI, 20.

OBJECT 10
Fragment, Grave 2643, Matmar
No image, similar to Figure 2. From G. Brunton, *Matmar*, (1948) London: B. Quaritch LTD.

OBJECT 11 (FIGURE 7)
Figurine, Grave 1832, Mostagedda
From G. Brunton, *Mostagedda and the Tasian Culture*, (1937), London: B. Quaritch LTD, PL. XLII, 6.

OBJECT 12 (FIGURE 8)
Figurine, Grave 1872, Mostagedda
From G. Brunton, *Mostagedda and the Tasian Culture*, (1937), London: B. Quaritch LTD, PL. XLII, 2.

OBJECT 13
Fragment, Grave H.33, El-Mahasna
No image, only description: '...the legs of a very large steatophygous clay figure painted red', E. R. Ayrton and W. L. S. Loat, *Predynastic Cemetery at El-Mahasna*, (1911), London: Egypt Exploration Fund, 14.

OBJECT 14
Fragment, Grave H.42, El-Mahasna
No image, only description: '...the remains of a clay female steatophygous figure which had crumbled to pieces', E. R. Ayrton and W. L. S. Loat, *Predynastic Cemetery at El-Mahasna*, (1911), London: Egypt Exploration Fund, 13.

OBJECT 15 (FIGURE 9)
Fragment, Grave H.97, El-Mahasna
From E. R. Ayrton and W. L. S. Loat, *Predynastic Cemetery at El-Mahasna*, (1911), London: Egypt Exploration Fund, Pl. XV, 1.

OBJECT 16
Fragment, Grave H.85, El-Mahasna
No image, only description: 'In the rubbish were a few fragments of clay painted red, which may have belonged to one of the steatophygous figures, such as was found in H.33', E. R. Ayrton and W. L. S. Loat, *Predynastic Cemetery at El-Mahasna*, (1911), London: Egypt Exploration Fund, 19.

OBJECT 17 (FIGURE 10)
Figurine, Grave H.29, El-Mahasna
From E. R. Ayrton and W. L. S. Loat, *Predynastic Cemetery at El-Mahasna*, (1911), London: Egypt Exploration Fund, Pl. XI, 1.

OBJECT 18
Fragment, Grave H.29, El-Mahasna
No image, only description: 'Just at the back of the shoulder blades of this skeleton were two large pieces of clay, painted red, but too broken to be examined, which may perhaps have originally formed part of a clay steatophygous figure', E. R. Ayrton and W. L. S. Loat, *Predynastic Cemetery at El-Mahasna*, (1911), London: Egypt Exploration Fund, 12.

OBJECT 19
Fragment, Grave H.29, El-Mahasna
No image, only description, same as Figure 18.

APPENDIX IV - LIST OF OBJECTS AND FIGURES

OBJECT 20 (FIGURE 11)
Figurine, Grave H.41, El-Mahasna
From E. R. Ayrton and W. L. S. Loat, *Predynastic Cemetery at El-Mahasna*, (1911), London: Egypt Exploration Fund, Pl. XVI, 1.

OBJECT 21
Figurine, Grave A.41, El-Amrah
No image, only description: 'Small clay doll, with curly black hair and curly beard', D. R. MacIver and A. C. Mace, *El-Amrah and Abydos, 1899 – 1901*, (1903), London: Egypt Exploration Fund, 16.

OBJECT 22
Fragment, Grave A.57, El-Amrah
No image, only description: 'Fragments of baskets and a female doll', D. R. MacIver and A. C. Mace, *El-Amrah and Abydos, 1899 – 1901*, (1903), London: Egypt Exploration Fund, 16.

OBJECT 23
Figurine, Grave A.72, El-Amrah
No image, only description: 'Clay doll', D. R. MacIver and A. C. Mace, *El-Amrah and Abydos, 1899 – 1901*, (1903), London: Egypt Exploration Fund, 16.

OBJECT 24
Figurine, Grave A.74, El-Amrah
No image, only description: 'Female doll in red pottery', D. R. MacIver and A. C. Mace, *El-Amrah and Abydos, 1899 – 1901*, (1903), London: Egypt Exploration Fund, 23.

OBJECT 25
Fragment, Grave A.117, El-Amrah
No image, only description: 'Half the head of a clay doll', D. R. MacIver and A. C. Mace, *El-Amrah and Abydos, 1899 – 1901*, (1903), London: Egypt Exploration Fund, 24.

OBJECT 26
Fragment, Grave A.90, El-Amrah
No image, only description: 'Head of curly haired clay doll', D. R. MacIver and A. C. Mace, *El-Amrah and Abydos, 1899 – 1901*, (1903), London: Egypt Exploration Fund, 16.

OBJECT 27 (FIGURE 12)
Figurine, Grave A.56, El-Amrah
From D. R. MacIver and A. C. Mace, *El-Amrah and Abydos, 1899 – 1901*, (1903), London: Egypt Exploration Fund, Pl. IX, 11.

OBJECT 28 (FIGURE 12)
Figurine, Grave A.56, El-Amrah
From D. R. MacIver and A. C. Mace, *El-Amrah and Abydos, 1899 – 1901*, (1903), London: Egypt Exploration Fund, Pl. IX, 11.

OBJECT 29 (FIGURE 13)
Figurine, Grave A.94, El-Amrah
From D. R. MacIver and A. C. Mace, *El-Amrah and Abydos, 1899 – 1901*, (1903), London: Egypt Exploration Fund, Pl. IXV, 7.

EGYPTIAN PREDYNASTIC ANTHROPOMORPHIC OBJECTS

OBJECT 30
Fragment, Grave B.202, El-Amrah
No image, only description: 'Fragments of clay male doll, with grotesque punch-like head', D. R. MacIver and A. C. Mace, *El-Amrah and Abydos, 1899 – 1901*, (1903), London: Egypt Exploration Fund, 17.

OBJECT 31 (FIGURE 14)
Figurine, Grave B.83, Abadiya
From P. Ucko, *Anthropomorphic Figurines of Predynastic Egypt and Neolithic Crete with Comparative Material from the Prehistoric Near East and Mainland Greece*, (1968), Figure 6.

OBJECT 32 (FIGURE 15)
Figurine, Grave B.83, Abadiya
From P. Ucko, *Anthropomorphic Figurines of Predynastic Egypt and Neolithic Crete with Comparative Material from the Prehistoric Near East and Mainland Greece*, (1968),), London: Andrew Szmilda, Figure 7.

OBJECT 33 (FIGURE 16)
Figurine, Grave B.83, Abadiya
From P. Ucko, *Anthropomorphic Figurines of Predynastic Egypt and Neolithic Crete with Comparative Material from the Prehistoric Near East and Mainland Greece*, (1968), London: Andrew Szmilda, Figure 5.

OBJECT 34 (FIGURE 17)
Figurine, Grave B.83, Abadiya
From D. C. Patch, *Dawn of Egyptian Art*, (2011), London: The Metropolitan Museum of Art, Cat. 84,105.

OBJECT 35 (FIGURE 18)
Figurine, Grave B.83, Abadiya
From J. C. Payne, *Catalogue of the Predynastic Egyptian Collection in the Ashmolean Museum*, (1993), Oxford: Oxford University Press, Fig. 6.27.

OBJECT 36 (FIGURE 18)
Figurine, Grave B.83, Abadiya
From J. C. Payne, *Catalogue of the Predynastic Egyptian Collection in the Ashmolean Museum*, (1993), Oxford: Oxford University Press, Fig. 6.27.

OBJECT 37 (FIGURE 19)
Figurine, Grave B.101, Abadiya
From J. C. Payne, *Catalogue of the Predynastic Egyptian Collection in the Ashmolean Museum*, (1993), Oxford: Oxford University Press, Fig. 9.33.

OBJECT 38 (FIGURE 20)
Figurine, Grave B.101, Abadiya
From J. C. Payne, *Catalogue of the Predynastic Egyptian Collection in the Ashmolean Museum*, (1993), Oxford: Oxford University Press, Fig. 9.35.

OBJECT 39 (FIGURE 21)
Figurine, Grave B.101, Abadiya
From J. C. Payne, *Catalogue of the Predynastic Egyptian Collection in the Ashmolean Museum*, (1993), Oxford: Oxford University Press, Fig. 9.34.

APPENDIX IV - LIST OF OBJECTS AND FIGURES

OBJECT 40 (FIGURE 22)
Fragment, Grave B101, Abadiya
From J. C. Payne, *Catalogue of the Predynastic Egyptian Collection in the Ashmolean Museum*, (1993), Oxford: Oxford University Press, Fig. 9.36.

OBJECT 41 (FIGURE 23)
Fragment, Grave B101, Abadiya
From J. C. Payne, *Catalogue of the Predynastic Egyptian Collection in the Ashmolean Museum*, (1993), Oxford: Oxford University Press, Fig. 12.45.

OBJECT 42 (FIGURE 24)
Fragment, Grave B101, Abadiya
From J. C. Payne, *Catalogue of the Predynastic Egyptian Collection in the Ashmolean Museum*, (1993), Oxford: Oxford University Press, Fig. 12.51.

OBJECT 43 (FIGURE 25)
Vessel, Grave B102, Abadiya
From J. C. Payne, *Catalogue of the Predynastic Egyptian Collection in the Ashmolean Museum*, (1993), Oxford: Oxford University Press, Fig. 31.574.

OBJECT 44 (FIGURE 26)
Figurine, Grave B.109, Abadiya
From Patch, D. C., *Dawn of Egyptian Art*, (2011), London: The Metropolitan Museum of Art, 116, Cat.95.

OBJECT 45 (FIGURE 27)
Figurine, Grave B119, Abadiya
From J. C. Payne, *Catalogue of the Predynastic Egyptian Collection in the Ashmolean Museum*, (1993), Oxford: Oxford University Press, Fig. 12.48.

OBJECT 46 (FIGURE 28)
Figurine, Grave B119, Abadiya
From J. C. Payne, *Catalogue of the Predynastic Egyptian Collection in the Ashmolean Museum*, (1993), Oxford: Oxford University Press, Fig. 10.41.

OBJECT 47 (FIGURE 29)
Figurine, Grave 394, Abadiya
From J. C. Payne, *Catalogue of the Predynastic Egyptian Collection in the Ashmolean Museum*, (1993), Oxford: Oxford University Press, Fig. 11.42.

OBJECT 48 (FIGURE 30)
Tag, Grave T4, Naqada
From W. M. F. Petrie, *Naqada and Ballas*, (1896), London: B. Quaritch LTD, Pl. LIX, 2.

OBJECT 49 (FIGURE 30)
Tag, Grave T4, Naqada
From W. M. F. Petrie, *Naqada and Ballas*, (1896), London: B. Quaritch LTD, Pl. LIX, 2.

OBJECT 50 (FIGURE 30)
Tag, Grave T4, Naqada
From W. M. F. Petrie, *Naqada and Ballas*, (1896), London: B. Quaritch LTD, Pl. LIX, 2.

OBJECT 51 (FIGURE 31)
Tusk, Grave T4, Naqada
From J. C. Payne, *Catalogue of the Predynastic Egyptian Collection in the Ashmolean Museum*, (1993), Oxford: Oxford University Press, Fig. 81.1965.

OBJECT 52 (FIGURE 32)
Tag, Grave T24, Naqada
From J. C. Payne, *Catalogue of the Predynastic Egyptian Collection in the Ashmolean Museum*, (1993), Oxford: Oxford University Press, Fig. 81.1962.

OBJECT 53 (FIGURE 33)
Tusk, Grave 226, Naqada
From J. C. Payne, *Catalogue of the Predynastic Egyptian Collection in the Ashmolean Museum*, (1993), Oxford: Oxford University Press, Fig. 81.1964.

OBJECT 54 (FIGURE 34)
Comb, Grave 268, Naqada
From J. C. Payne, *Catalogue of the Predynastic Egyptian Collection in the Ashmolean Museum*, (1993), Oxford: Oxford University Press, Fig. 77.1900.

OBJECT 55 (FIGURE 35)
Figurine, Grave 271, Naqada
From J. C. Payne, *Catalogue of the Predynastic Egyptian Collection in the Ashmolean Museum*, (1993), Oxford: Oxford University Press, Fig. 3.8.

OBJECT 56 (FIGURE 36)
Figurine, Grave 271, Naqada
From B. Adams, *Predynastic Egypt*, (1988), Shire: Princess Risborough,55, Fig. 36, 1.

OBJECT 57 (FIGURE 37)
Figurine, Grave 271, Naqada
From B. Adams, *Predynastic Egypt*, (1988), Shire: Princess Risborough,55, Fig. 36, 3.

OBJECT 58 (FIGURE 38)
Fragment, Grave 271, Naqada
From B. Adams, *Predynastic Egypt*, (1988), Shire: Princess Risborough, 55, Fig. 36, 2.

OBJECT 59 (FIGURE 39)
Figurine, Grave 271, Naqada
From J. C. Payne, *Catalogue of the Predynastic Egyptian Collection in the Ashmolean Museum*, (1993), Oxford: Oxford University Press, Fig. 8.30.

OBJECT 60 (FIGURE 40)
Tag, Grave 271, Naqada
From J. C. Payne, *Catalogue of the Predynastic Egyptian Collection in the Ashmolean Museum*, (1993), Oxford: Oxford University Press, Fig. 81.1960.

APPENDIX IV - LIST OF OBJECTS AND FIGURES

OBJECT 61 (FIGURE 41)
Fragment, Grave 273, Naqada
From J. C. Payne, *Catalogue of the Predynastic Egyptian Collection in the Ashmolean Museum*, (1993), Oxford: Oxford University Press, Fig. 3. 10.

OBJECT 62 (FIGURE 42)
Tag, Grave 276, Naqada.
From W. M. F. Petrie, *Naqada and Ballas*, (1896), London: B. Quaritch LTD, Pl. LIX, 8.

OBJECT 63 (FIGURE 42)
Tag, Grave 276, Naqada.
From W. M. F. Petrie, *Naqada and Ballas*, (1896), London: B. Quaritch LTD, Pl. LIX, 8.

OBJECT 64 (FIGURE 42)
Tag, Grave 276, Naqada
From W. M. F. Petrie, *Naqada and Ballas*, (1896), London: B. Quaritch LTD, Pl. LIX, 8.

OBJECT 65 (FIGURE 43)
Tag, Grave 1329, Naqada
From W. M. F. Petrie, *Naqada and Ballas*, (1896), London: B. Quaritch LTD, Pl. LIX, 3.

OBJECT 66 (FIGURE 44)
Tag, Grave 1329, Naqada
From J. C. Payne, *Catalogue of the Predynastic Egyptian Collection in the Ashmolean Museum*, (1993), Oxford: Oxford University Press, Fig. 81. 1959.

OBJECT 67 (FIGURE 45)
Comb, Grave 1411, Naqada
From J. C. Payne, *Catalogue of the Predynastic Egyptian Collection in the Ashmolean Museum*, (1993), Oxford: Oxford University Press, Fig. 77.1901.

OBJECT 68 (FIGURE 46)
Fragment, Grave 1413, Naqada
From UCL Petrie Museum Catalogue, UC4600.
http://petriecat.museums.ucl.ac.uk, accessed on 10th January, 2016.
Reproduced with permission of the Petrie Museum.

OBJECT 69 (FIGURE 47)
Fragment, Grave 1413, Naqada
From UCL Petrie Museum Catalogue, UC4601.
http://petriecat.museums.ucl.ac.uk, accessed on 10th January, 2016.
Reproduced with permission of the Petrie Museum.

OBJECT 70 (FIGURE 48)
Tusk, Grave 1419, Naqada
From W. M. F. Petrie, *Naqada and Ballas*, (1896), London: B. Quaritch LTD, Pl. LXII, 34.

OBJECT 71 (FIGURE 48)
Tag, Grave 1419, Naqada
From W. M. F. Petrie, *Naqada and Ballas*, (1896), London: B. Quaritch LTD, Pl. LXII, 34.

OBJECT 72 (FIGURE 49)
Figurine, Grave 1488, Naqada
From J. C. Payne, *Catalogue of the Predynastic Egyptian Collection in the Ashmolean Museum*, (1993), Oxford: Oxford University Press, Fig. 8. 31.

OBJECT 73 (FIGURE 50)
Figurine, Grave 1488, Naqada
From J. C. Payne, *Catalogue of the Predynastic Egyptian Collection in the Ashmolean Museum*, (1993), Oxford: Oxford University Press, Fig. 8. 32.

OBJECT 74 (FIGURE 51)
Fragment, Grave 1503, Naqada
From J. C. Payne, *Catalogue of the Predynastic Egyptian Collection in the Ashmolean Museum*, (1993), Oxford: Oxford University Press, Fig. 10. 40.

OBJECT 75 (FIGURE 52)
Figurine, Grave 1530, Naqada
From UCL Petrie Museum Catalogue, UC4580.
http://petriecat.museums.ucl.ac.uk, accessed on 10th January, 2016.
Reproduced with permission of the Petrie Museum.

OBJECT 76 (FIGURE 53)
Fragment, Grave 1530, Naqada
From UCL Petrie Museum Catalogue, UC4581.
http://petriecat.museums.ucl.ac.uk, accessed on 10th January, 2016.
Reproduced with permission of the Petrie Museum.

OBJECT 77 (FIGURE 54)
Fragment, Grave 1546, Naqada
From UCL Petrie Museum Catalogue, UC5075.
http://petriecat.museums.ucl.ac.uk, accessed on 10th January, 2016.
Reproduced with permission of the Petrie Museum.

OBJECT 78 (FIGURE 55)
Fragment, Grave 1546, Naqada
From UCL Petrie Museum Catalogue, UC5076.
http://petriecat.museums.ucl.ac.uk, accessed on 10th January, 2016.
Reproduced with permission of the Petrie Museum.

OBJECT 79 (FIGURE 56)
Comb, Grave 1561, Naqada
From UCL Petrie Museum Catalogue, UC4600.
http://petriecat.museums.ucl.ac.uk, accessed on 10th January, 2016.
Reproduced with permission of the Petrie Museum.

OBJECT 80 (FIGURE 57)
Tag, Grave 1583, Naqada
From UCL Petrie Museum Catalogue, UC4606.
http://petriecat.museums.ucl.ac.uk, accessed on 10th January, 2016.
Reproduced with permission of the Petrie Museum.

APPENDIX IV - LIST OF OBJECTS AND FIGURES

OBJECT 81 (FIGURE 58)
Figurine, Grave 1611, Naqada
From J. C. Payne, *Catalogue of the Predynastic Egyptian Collection in the Ashmolean Museum*, (1993), Oxford: Oxford University Press, Fig. 10. 39.

OBJECT 82 (FIGURE 59)
Figurine, Grave 1687, Naqada
From J. C. Payne, *Catalogue of the Predynastic Egyptian Collection in the Ashmolean Museum*, (1993), Oxford: Oxford University Press, Fig. 8. 29.

OBJECT 83 (FIGURE 60)
Figurine, Grave 1677, Naqada
From UCL Petrie Museum Catalogue, UC4464.
http://petriecat.museums.ucl.ac.uk, accessed on 10th January, 2016.
Reproduced with permission of the Petrie Museum.

OBJECT 84 (FIGURE 61)
Fragment, Grave 1705, Naqada
From UCL Petrie Museum Catalogue, UC5363.
http://petriecat.museums.ucl.ac.uk, accessed on 10th January, 2016.
Reproduced with permission of the Petrie Museum.

OBJECT 85 (FIGURE 62)
Tag, Grave 1757, Naqada
From UCL Petrie Museum Catalogue, UC5453.
http://petriecat.museums.ucl.ac.uk, accessed on 10th January, 2016.
Reproduced with permission of the Petrie Museum.

OBJECT 86 (FIGURE 63)
Tag, Grave 1757, Naqada
From UCL Petrie Museum Catalogue, UC5454.
http://petriecat.museums.ucl.ac.uk, accessed on 10th January, 2016.
Reproduced with permission of the Petrie Museum.

OBJECT 87 (FIGURE 64)
Tag, Grave 1757, Naqada
From UCL Petrie Museum Catalogue, UC5455.
http://petriecat.museums.ucl.ac.uk, accessed on 10th January, 2016.
Reproduced with permission of the Petrie Museum.

OBJECT 88 (FIGURE 65)
Fragment, Grave 1788, Naqada
From UCL Petrie Museum Catalogue, UC5077.
http://petriecat .museums.ucl.ac.uk, accessed on 10th January, 2016.
Reproduced with permission of the Petrie Museum.

OBJECT 89 (FIGURE 66)
Figurine, Grave 72, Hierakonpolis
From L. McNamara, (2014), 'The Ivory Statuette from HK6 Tomb 72', *Nekhen News*, 26, 8.

EGYPTIAN PREDYNASTIC ANTHROPOMORPHIC OBJECTS

OBJECT 90 (FIGURE 67)
Figurine, Grave 72, Hierakonpolis
From L. McNamara, (2014), 'The Ivory Statuette from HK6 Tomb 72', *Nekhen News*, 26, 17.

OBJECT 91 (FIGURE 68)
Tag, Grave B33, Hierakonpolis
From, R. Friedman, 'A Basket of Delights: The 2003 Excavations at HK43', *Nekhen News*, 15, 8.

OBJECT 92 (FIGURE 69)
Figurine, Grave U21, Abydos
From P. Ucko, *Anthropomorphic Figurines of Predynastic Egypt and Neolithic Crete with Comparative Material from the Prehistoric Near East and Mainland Greece*, (1968), London: Andrew Szmilda, Figure 49.

OBJECT 93 (FIGURE 70)
Vessel, Grave U 502, Abydos
From D. C. Patch, *Dawn of Egyptian Art*, (2011), London: The Metropolitan Museum of Art, Fig.34, 115.

OBJECT 94 (FIGURE 71)
Figurine, Grave U 502, Abydos
From Dreyer et. al., *Umm El-Qaab, Nachuntersuchungen Im Fruhzeitlichen Konigsfriedhof*, (1998), MDAIK, 56, 43-159; Abb. 12: 3.

OBJECT 95 (FIGURE 71)
Figurine, Grave U 502, Abydos
From Dreyer et. al., *Umm El-Qaab, Nachuntersuchungen Im Fruhzeitlichen Konigsfriedhof*, (1998), MDAIK, 56, 43-159; Abb. 12: 3.

OBJECT 96 (FIGURE 72)
Figurine, Grave 2, El-Ma'mariya
From 'Female Figure', Brooklyn Museum Online Collections, New York.
https://www.brooklynmuseum.org/opencollection/objects/4225
Accessed on 10th January, 2016. Reproduced with permission from the Brooklyn Museum, New York.

OBJECT 97 (FIGURE 73)
Figurine, Grave 2, El-Ma'mariya
From 'Female Figurine', Brooklyn Museum Online Collections, New York.
https://www.brooklynmuseum.org/opencollection/objects/4223
Accessed on 10th January, 2016. Reproduced with permission from the Brooklyn Museum, New York.

OBJECT 98 (FIGURE 74)
Figurine, Grave 186, El-Ma'mariya
From 'Female Figurine', Brooklyn Museum Online Collections, New York.
https://www.brooklynmuseum.org/opencollection/objects/123075
Accessed on 10th January, 2016. Reproduced with permission from the Brooklyn Museum, New York.

OBJECT 99 (FIGURE 75)
Figurine, Grave 186, El-Ma'mariya
From 'Figurine of Woman', Brooklyn Museum Online Collections, New York.
http://cdn2.brooklynmuseum.org/images/opencollection/objects/size3/07.447.504_SL1.jpg
Accessed on 10th January, 2016. Reproduced with permission from the Brooklyn Museum, New York.

APPENDIX IV - LIST OF OBJECTS AND FIGURES

OBJECT 100 (FIGURE 76)
Figurine, Grave 186, El-Ma'mariya
Image courtesy of Kathy Zurek-Doule, Curatorial Assistant – Egyptian, Classical, and Ancient Near Eastern Art. Reproduced with permission from the Brooklyn Museum, New York.

OBJECT 101 (FIGURE 77)
Figurine, Grave 186, El-Ma'mariya
Image courtesy of Kathy Zurek-Doule, Curatorial Assistant – Egyptian, Classical, and Ancient Near Eastern Art. Reproduced with permission from the Brooklyn Museum, New York.

OBJECT 102 (FIGURE 78)
Figurine, Grave 186, El-Ma'mariya
Image courtesy of Kathy Zurek-Doule, Curatorial Assistant – Egyptian, Classical, and Ancient Near Eastern Art. Reproduced with permission from the Brooklyn Museum, New York.

OBJECT 103 (FIGURE 79)
Figurine, Grave 186, El-Ma'mariya
Image courtesy of Kathy Zurek-Doule, Curatorial Assistant – Egyptian, Classical, and Ancient Near Eastern Art. Reproduced with permission from the Brooklyn Museum, New York.

OBJECT 104 (FIGURE 80)
Figurine, Grave 186, El-Ma'mariya
Image courtesy of Kathy Zurek-Doule, Curatorial Assistant – Egyptian, Classical, and Ancient Near Eastern Art. Reproduced with permission from the Brooklyn Museum, New York.

OBJECT 105 (FIGURE 81)
Figurine, Grave 186, El-Ma'mariya
Image courtesy of Kathy Zurek-Doule, Curatorial Assistant – Egyptian, Classical, and Ancient Near Eastern Art. Reproduced with permission from the Brooklyn Museum, New York.

OBJECT 106 (FIGURE 82)
Figurine, Grave 186, El-Ma'mariya
Image courtesy of Kathy Zurek-Doule, Curatorial Assistant – Egyptian, Classical, and Ancient Near Eastern Art. Reproduced with permission from the Brooklyn Museum, New York.

OBJECT 107 (FIGURE 83)
Figurine, Grave 186, El-Ma'mariya
Image courtesy of Kathy Zurek-Doule, Curatorial Assistant – Egyptian, Classical, and Ancient Near Eastern Art. Reproduced with permission from the Brooklyn Museum, New York.

OBJECT 108 (FIGURE 84)
Figurine, Grave 186, El-Ma'mariya
Image courtesy of Kathy Zurek-Doule, Curatorial Assistant – Egyptian, Classical, and Ancient Near Eastern Art. Reproduced with permission from the Brooklyn Museum, New York.

OBJECT 109 (FIGURE 85)
Figurine, Grave 186, El-Ma'mariya.
Image courtesy of Kathy Zurek-Doule, Curatorial Assistant – Egyptian, Classical, and Ancient Near Eastern Art. Reproduced with permission from the Brooklyn Museum, New York.

EGYPTIAN PREDYNASTIC ANTHROPOMORPHIC OBJECTS

OBJECT 110 (FIGURE 86)
Figurine, Grave 186, El-Ma'mariya
Image courtesy of Kathy Zurek-Doule, Curatorial Assistant – Egyptian, Classical, and Ancient Near Eastern Art. Reproduced with permission from the Brooklyn Museum, New York.

OBJECT 111 (FIGURE 87)
Figurine, Grave 186, El-Ma'mariya
Image courtesy of Kathy Zurek-Doule, Curatorial Assistant – Egyptian, Classical, and Ancient Near Eastern Art. Reproduced with permission from the Brooklyn Museum, New York.

OBJECT 112 (FIGURE 88)
Figurine, Grave 186, El-Ma'mariya
Image courtesy of Kathy Zurek-Doule, Curatorial Assistant – Egyptian, Classical, and Ancient Near Eastern Art. Reproduced with permission from the Brooklyn Museum, New York.

OBJECT 113 (FIGURE 89)
Fragment, Grave 186, El-Ma'mariya
Image courtesy of Kathy Zurek-Doule, Curatorial Assistant – Egyptian, Classical, and Ancient Near Eastern Art. Reproduced with permission from the Brooklyn Museum, New York.

OBJECT 114 (FIGURE 90)
Fragment, Grave 186, El-Ma'mariya
Image courtesy of Kathy Zurek-Doule, Curatorial Assistant – Egyptian, Classical, and Ancient Near Eastern Art. Reproduced with permission from the Brooklyn Museum, New York.

OBJECT 115 (FIGURE 91)
Fragment, Grave 186, El-Ma'mariya
Image courtesy of Kathy Zurek-Doule, Curatorial Assistant – Egyptian, Classical, and Ancient Near Eastern Art. Reproduced with permission from the Brooklyn Museum, New York.

OBJECT 116 (FIGURE 92)
Fragment, Grave 186, El-Ma'mariya
Image courtesy of Kathy Zurek-Doule, Curatorial Assistant – Egyptian, Classical, and Ancient Near Eastern Art. Reproduced with permission from the Brooklyn Museum, New York.

OBJECT 117 (FIGURE 93)
Fragment, Grave 186, El-Ma'mariya
Image courtesy of Kathy Zurek-Doule, Curatorial Assistant – Egyptian, Classical, and Ancient Near Eastern Art. Reproduced with permission from the Brooklyn Museum, New York.

OBJECT 118 (FIGURE 94)
Fragment, Grave 186, El-Ma'mariya
Image courtesy of Kathy Zurek-Doule, Curatorial Assistant – Egyptian, Classical, and Ancient Near Eastern Art. Reproduced with permission from the Brooklyn Museum, New York.

FIGURE 95
Figurine, unprovenanced
From D. C. Patch, *Dawn of Egyptian Art*, (2011), London: The Metropolitan Museum of Art, Cat. 97, 117.

APPENDIX IV - LIST OF OBJECTS AND FIGURES

FIGURE 96
Figurines and stand, unprovenanced
From D. C. Patch, *Dawn of Egyptian Art*, (2011), London: The Metropolitan Museum of Art, Cat. 96, 116.
Ägyptisches Museum und Papyrussammlung Berlin, Inv.-Nr. ÄM 22700
© SMB Ägyptisches Museum und Papyrussammlung Berlin, photograph: S. Steiß

FIGURE 97
Grave 271 Plan, Naqada
From W. M. F. Petrie, *Naqada and Ballas*, (1896), London: B. Quaritch LTD, Pl. LXXIII.

FIGURE 98
Grave A.56 Plan, El-Amrah
From D. R. MacIver and A. C. Mace, *El Amrah and Abydos, 1899-1901*, (1902), London: Egypt Exploration Fund, PL. V, 8

FIGURE 99
Clay mask, HK6, Hierakonpolis
From R. Friedman, 'Discoveries in the Predynastic Cemetery at HK6 during the 2014 Season', Hierakonpolis Expedition website, http://www.hierakonpolis-online.org/index.php/explore-the-predynastic-cemeteries/hk6-elite-cemetery/tomb-72
Accessed on 22nd January, 2016.

FIGURE 100
Objects broken below the waist, with only the lower body remaining.
Drawings by the author.

FIGURE 101
Objects and fragments broken one or more times along the legs of the body.
Drawings by the author.

FIGURES

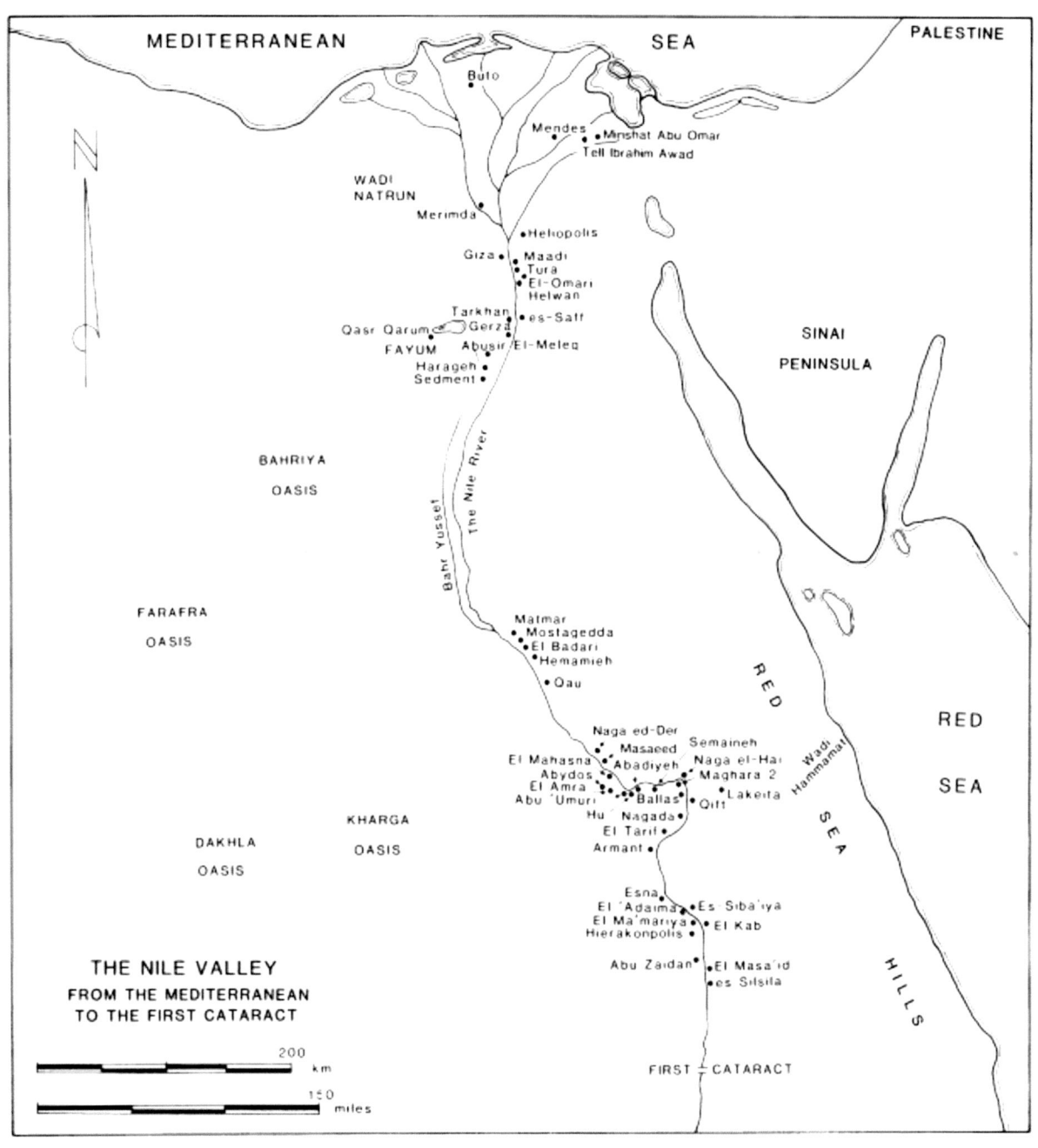

Figure 1

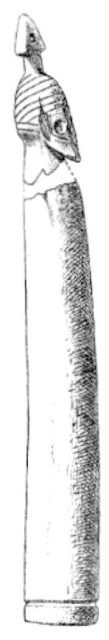

Figure 2

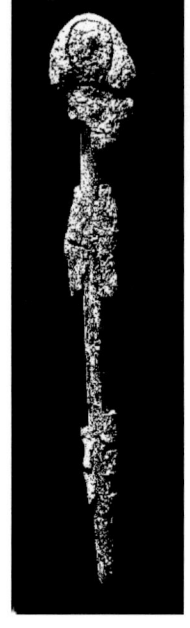

Figure 3

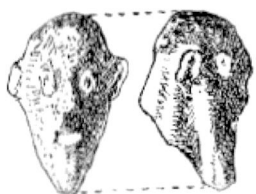

Figure 4

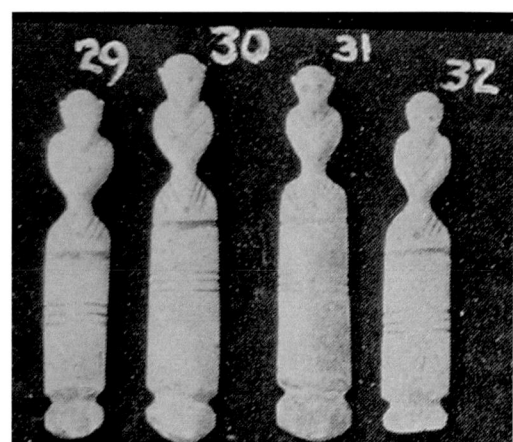

Figure 5

Figure 6

FIGURES

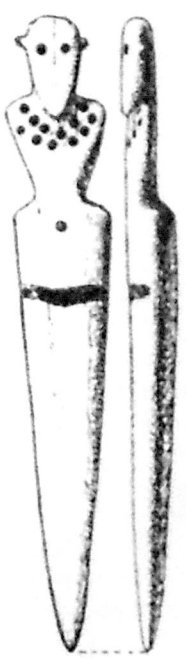

Figure 7

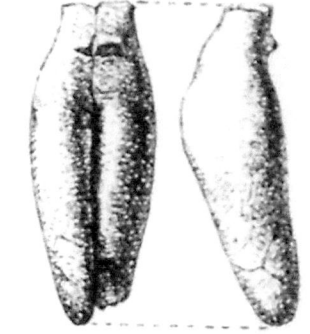

Figure 8

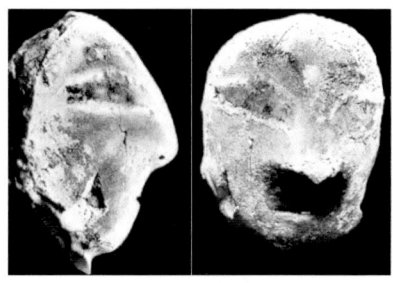

Figure 9

Figure 10

Figure 11

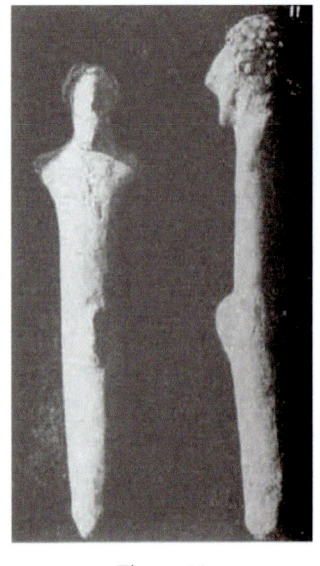

Figure 12

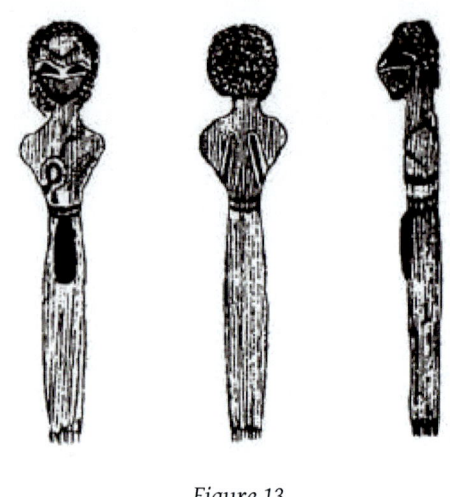

Figure 13

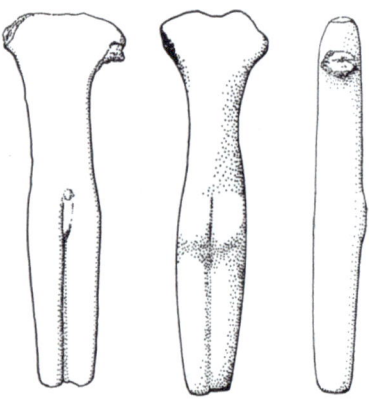

Figure 14

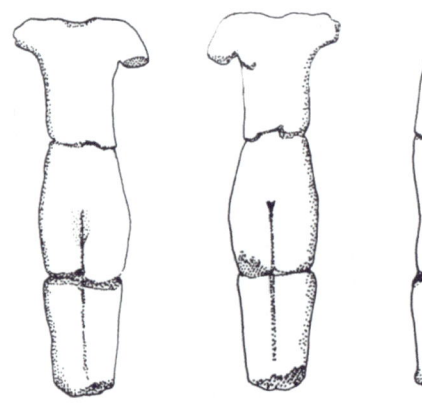

Figure 15

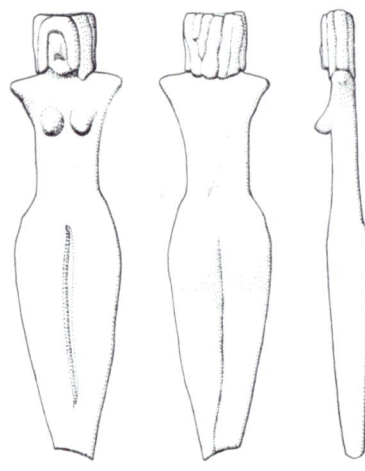

Figure 16

Figure 17

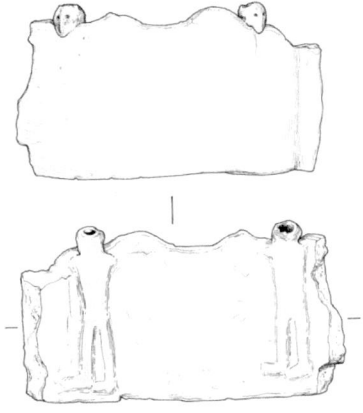

Figure 18

Figure 19

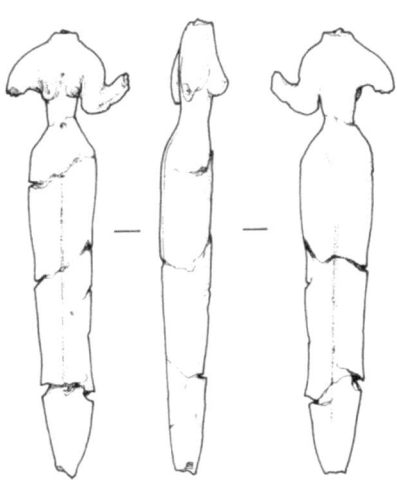

Figure 20

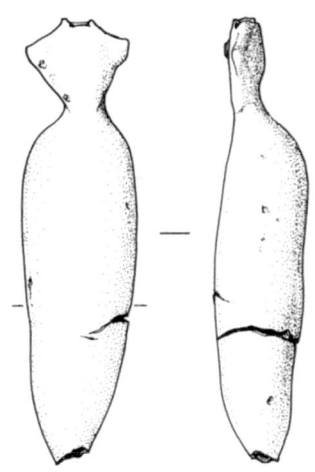

Figure 21

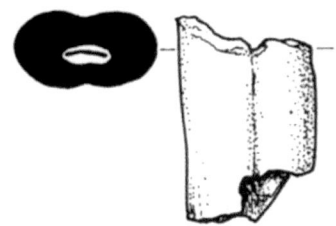

Figure 22

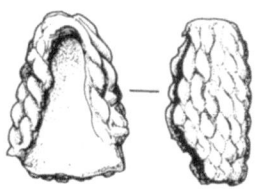

Figure 23

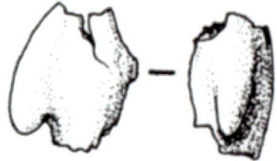

Figure 24

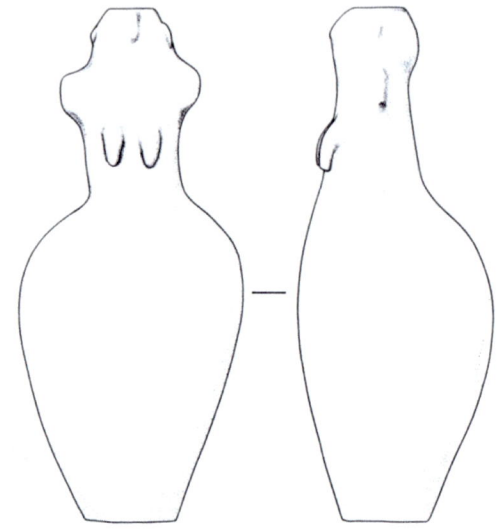

Figure 25

Figure 26

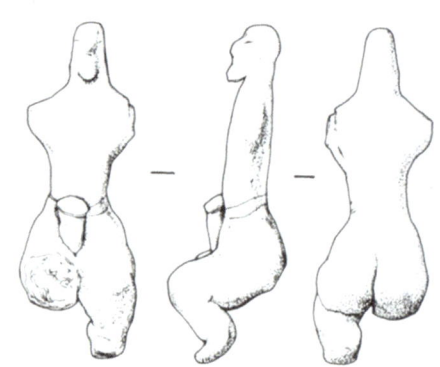

Figure 27

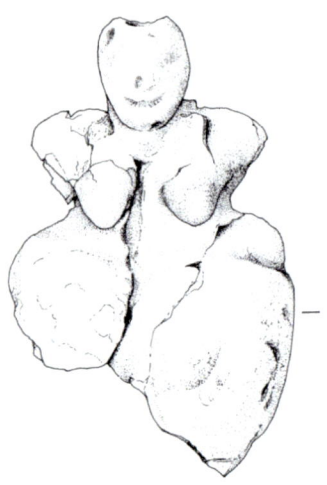

Figure 28

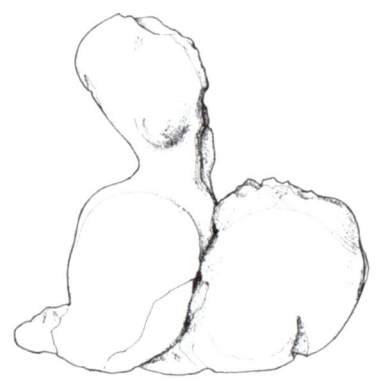

Figure 29

FIGURES

Figure 30

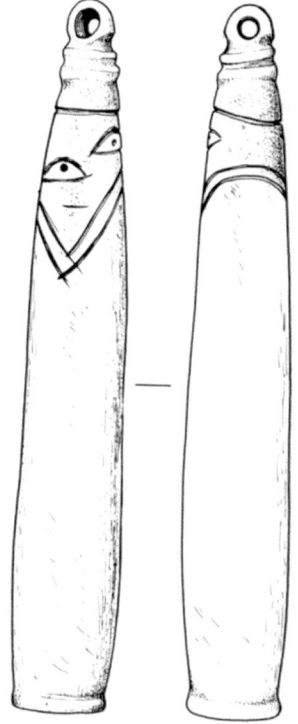

Figure 31

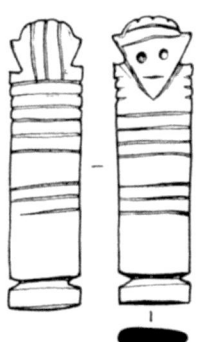

Figure 32

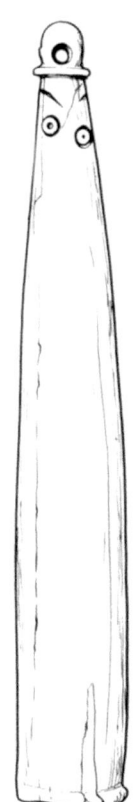

Figure 34

Figure 33

97

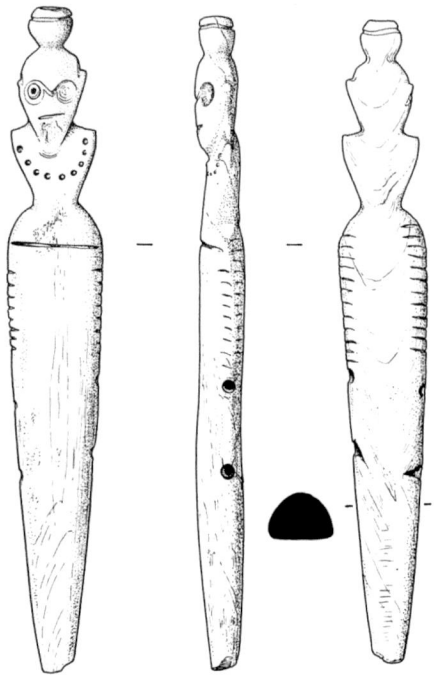

Figure 35

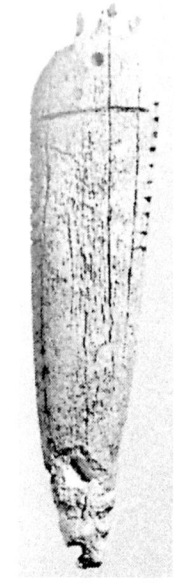

Figure 36

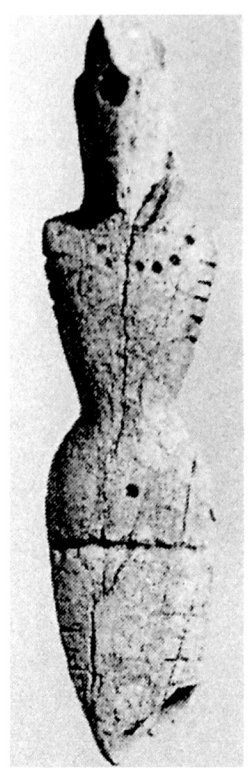

Figure 37

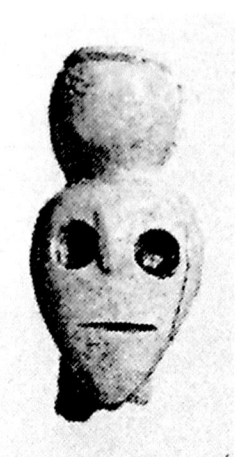

Figure 38

FIGURES

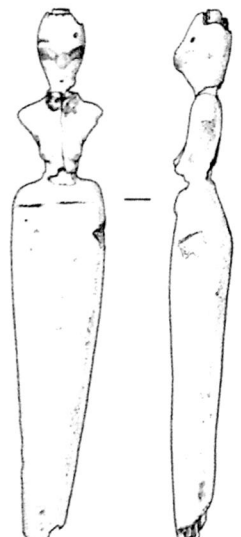

Figure 39

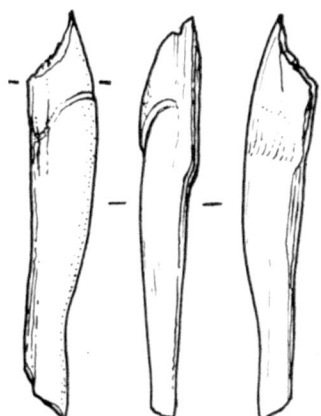

Figure 41

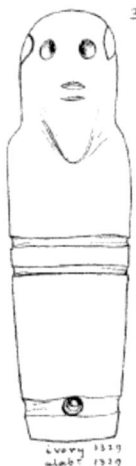

Figure 43

Figure 40

Figures 42

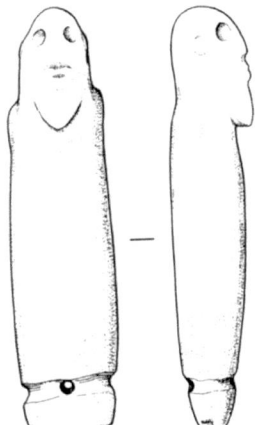

Figure 44

99

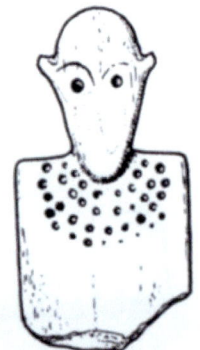

Figure 45

Figure 46

Figure 47

Figure 48

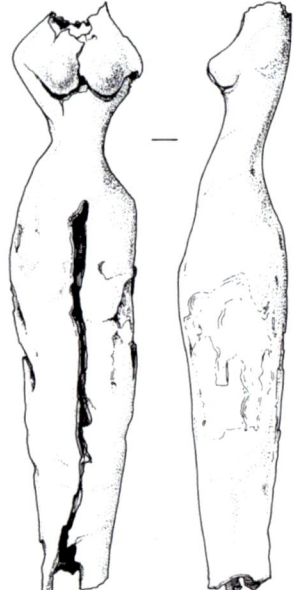

Figure 49

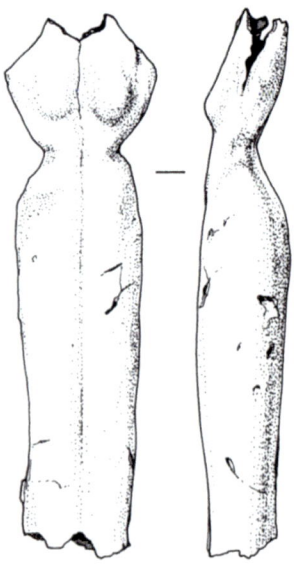

Figure 50

FIGURES

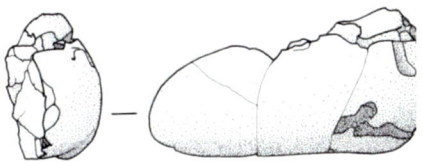

Figure 51

Figure 52

Figure 53

Figure 54

Figure 55

Figure 56

Figure 57

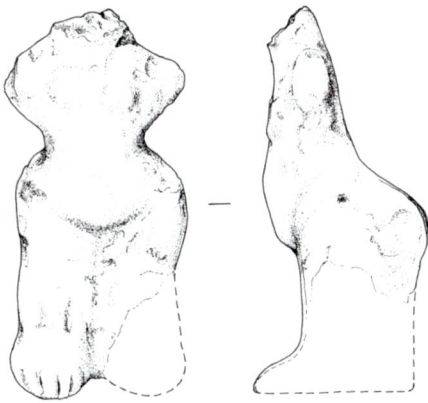

Figure 58

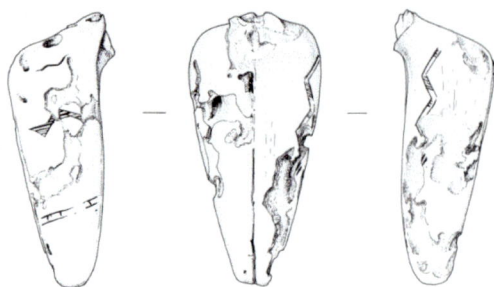

Figure 59

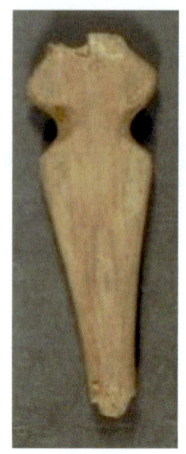

Figure 60

Figure 61.

Figure 62

Figure 63

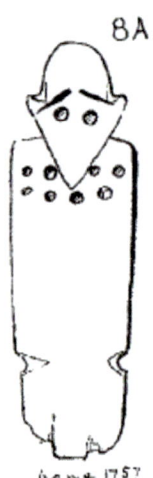

Figure 64

Figure 65

Figure 66

Figure 67

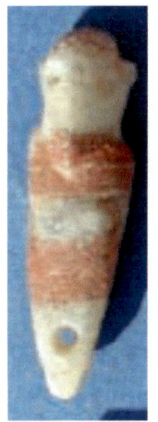

Figure 68

Figure 69

Figure 70

EGYPTIAN PREDYNASTIC ANTHROPOMORPHIC OBJECTS

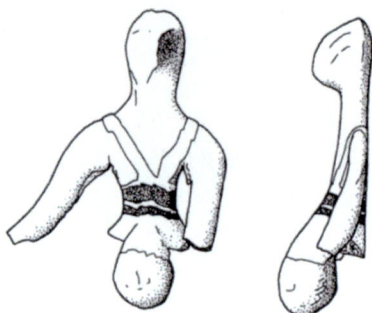

Figures 71

Figure 73

Figure 75

Figure 72

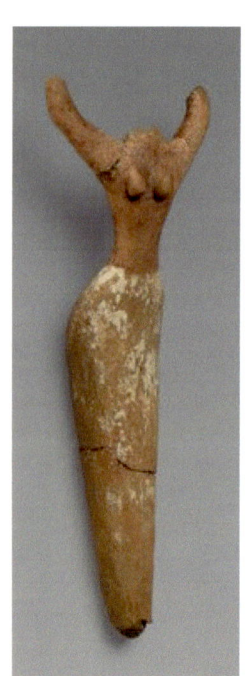

Figure 74

FIGURES

Figure 76

Figure 77

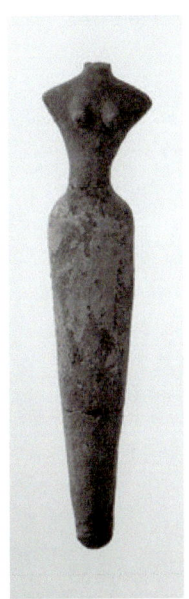

Figure 78

Figure 79

Figure 80

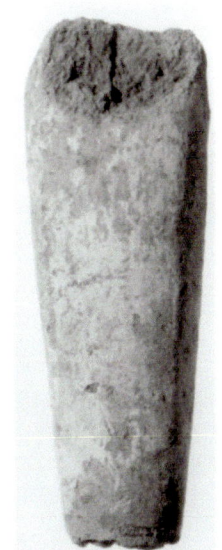

Figure 81

105

EGYPTIAN PREDYNASTIC ANTHROPOMORPHIC OBJECTS

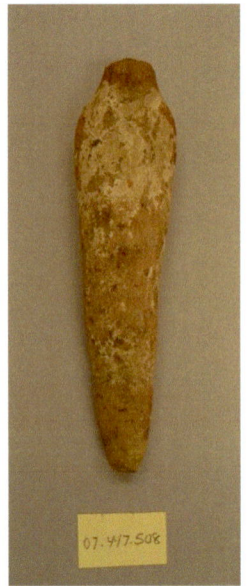

Figure 82

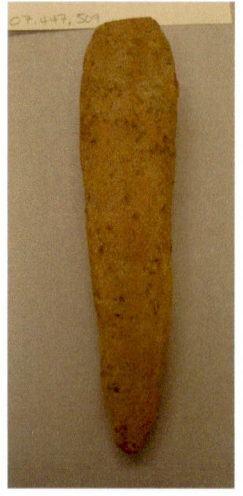

Figure 83

Figure 84

Figure 85

Figure 86

Figure 87

FIGURES

Figure 88

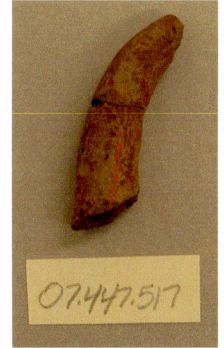

Figure 89

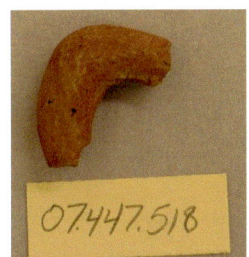

Figure 90

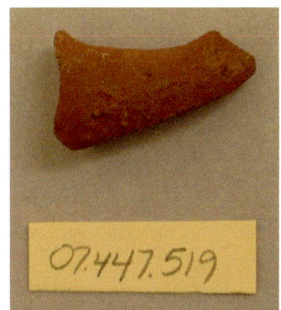

Figure 91

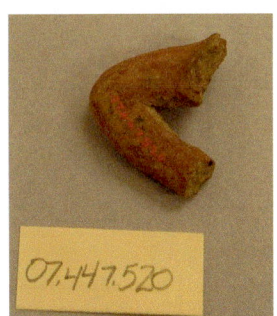

Figure 92

Figure 93

Figure 94

EGYPTIAN PREDYNASTIC ANTHROPOMORPHIC OBJECTS

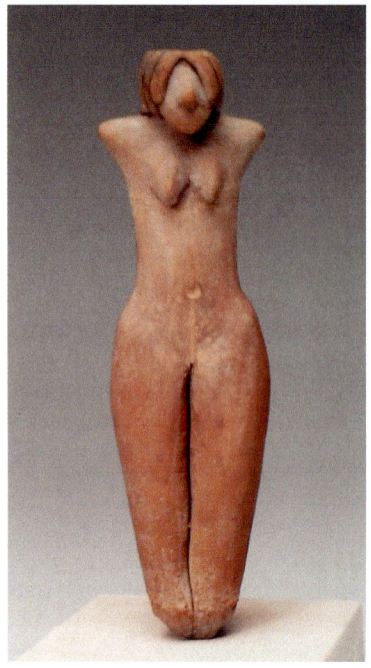

Figure 95

Figure 96

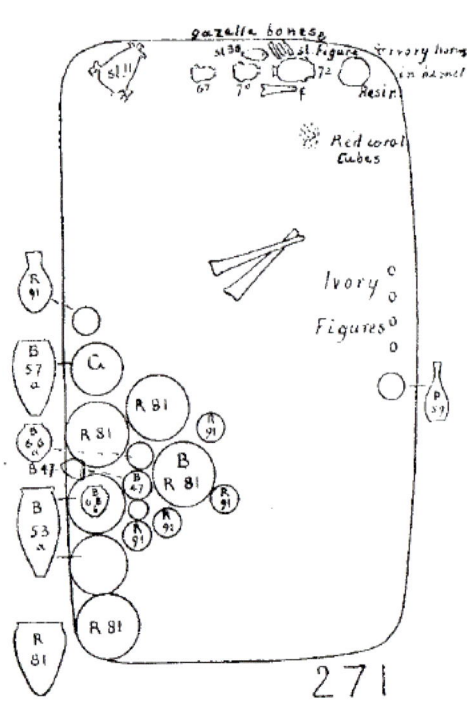

Figure 97

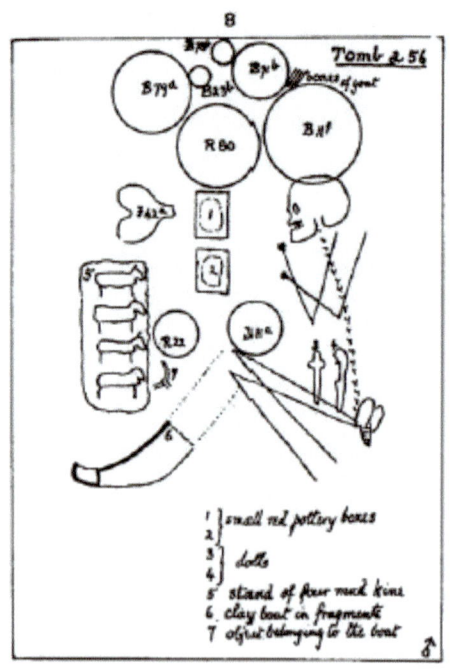

Figure 98

FIGURES

Figure 99

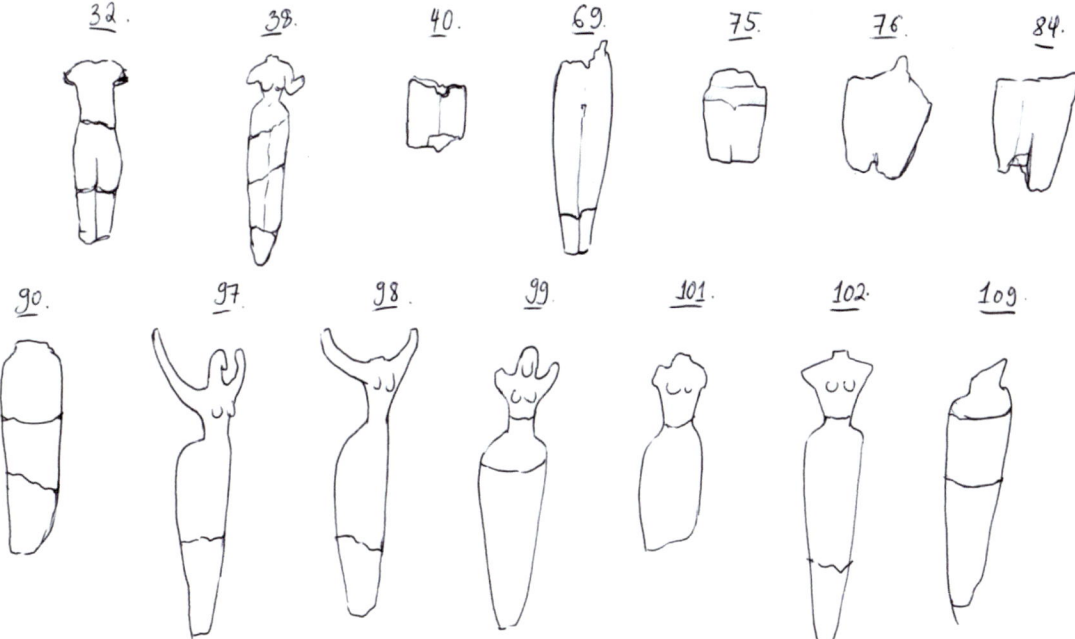

Figure 100

109

EGYPTIAN PREDYNASTIC ANTHROPOMORPHIC OBJECTS

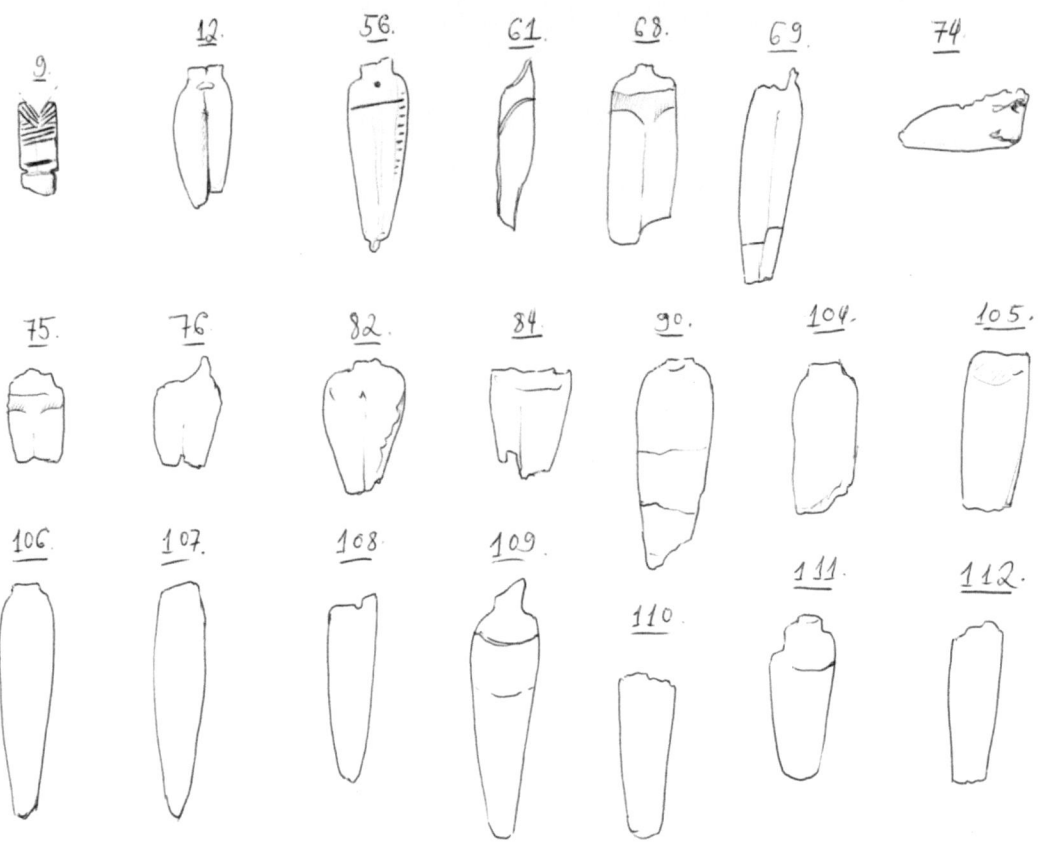

Figure 101

BIBLIOGRAPHY

ADAMS, B.,
(2002) 'Seeking the Roots of Ancient Egypt: A Unique Cemetery Reveals Monuments and Rituals from Before the Pharaohs', *Archeo-Nil*, 12, 11-28.
(2004) 'Excavations in the Elite Predynastic Cemetery at Hierakonpolis Locality HK6: 1999-2000', *Annales du Service des Antiques de l'Egypte*, 78, 35-52.

ALVAREZ, C. M. D. R. & ROSALES, E. A.,
(2004) 'An Analysis of the Theriomorphic Representations on Combs and Hairpins from the Predynastic Period', in S. Hendrickx, R.F. Friedman, K.M. Cialowicz and M. Chlodnicki (eds), *Egypt At Its Origins: Studies in Memory of Barbara Adam, Proceedings of the International Conference 'Origin of the State. Predynastic and Early Dynastic Egypt', Krakow, 28th August - 1st September 2002*, Leuven: Peeters, 881-889.

ANDELKOVIC, B.,
(2011) 'Political Organisation of Egypt in the Predynastic Period'. in E. Teeter (ed), *Before the Pyramids: The Origins of Egyptian Civilization*, Oriental Institute Museum Publications, Chicago: The Oriental Institute of the University of Chicago, 25-32.

ANDERSON, A. D.,
(2006) *Power and Competition in the Upper Egyptian Predynastic: A View from the Predynastic Settlement at el-Mahasna*, PhD Dissertation, University of Pittsburgh: University Microfilm International, Ann Arbor.
(2011) 'Evidence for Early Ritual Activity in the Predynastic Settlement at el-Mahasna', in R.F. Friedman and P.N. Fiske (eds), *Egypt At Its Origins 3: Proceedings of the Third International Conference 'Origin of the State. Predynastic and Early Dynastic Egypt', London, 27th July – 1st August 2008*, Leuven: OLA 205, 3-30.

ANDERSON, W.,
(1992) 'Badarian Burials: Evidence of Social Inequality in Middle Egypt during the Early Predynastic Era', *Journal of the American Research Center in Egypt*, 29, 51-66.

APPADURAI, A.,
(1986) 'Introduction: Commodities and the Politics of Value', in A. Appadurai (ed), *The Social Life of Things: Commodities in Cultural Perspective*, Cambridge: Cambridge University Press, 3-63.

ASTON, B. G., HARRELL, J. A. & SHAW, I.,
(2000) 'Stone', in P.T. Nicholson and I. Shaw (eds), *Ancient Egyptian Materials and Technology*, Cambridge: Cambridge University Press, 5-77.

AYRTON, E. R., & LOAT, W. L. S.,
(1911) *Pre-dynastic Cemetery at El Mahasna*, London: Egypt Explorations Fund.

BAILEY, D. W.,
(1994) 'Reading Prehistoric Figurines as Individuals', *World Archaeology*, 25, 321-331.
(2005) *Prehistoric Figurines: Representations and Corporeality in the Neolithic*, London: Routledge.
(2007) 'The Anti-Rhetorical Power of Representational Absence: Faceless Figurines in the Balkan Neolithic', in C. Renfrew and I. Morley (eds), *Material Beginnings: A Global Prehistory of Figurative Representation*, Cambridge: McDonald Institute for Archaeological Research, 117-126.
(2013) 'Figurines, Corporeality, and the Origins of the Gendered Body', in D. Bolger (ed), *A Companion to Gender Prehistory*, Oxford: Wiley-Blackwell, 244-264.

BARD, K.,
(1992) 'Toward an Interpretation of the Role of Ideology in the Evolution of Complex Society in Egypt', *Journal of Anthropological Archaeology*, 11, 1-24.
(1994) 'The Egyptian Predynastic: an Overview', *Journal of Field Archaeology*, 21, 265-288.
(2001) *From Farmers to Pharaohs: Mortuary Evidence for the Rise of Complex Society in Egypt*, Sheffield: Sheffield University Press.

BARLEY, N.,
(1994) *Smashing Pots: Feats of Clay from Africa*, London: British Museum Press.

BAUMGARTEL, E.,
(1955) *The Cultures of Prehistoric Egypt: Volume I*, London: Oxford University Press.
(1960) *The Cultures of Prehistoric Egypt: Volume II*, London: Oxford University Press.
(1970) 'Predynastic Egypt', in I.E.S. Edwards, C.J. Gadd and N.G.L. Hammond (eds), *Cambridge Ancient History: Volume I*, Cambridge: Cambridge University Press, 463-494.

BENTLEY, G. R.,
(1996) 'How Did Prehistoric Women Bear 'Man the Hunter'? Reconstructing Fertility from the Archaeological Record', in R.P. Wright (ed), *Gender and Archaeology: Essays in Research and Practice*, Philadelphia: University of Pennsylvania Press, 23-51.

BERNS, M. C.,
(1990) 'Pots and People: Yungur Ancestral Portraits', *African Arts*, 23, 50-60.
(1993) 'Art, History and Gender: Women and Clay in West Africa', *The African Archaeological Review*, 11, 129-148.

BINFORD, L. R.,
(1971) 'Mortuary Practices: Their Study and Potential', *Memoirs of the Society for American Archaeology*, 25, 6-29.

BOIVIN, N.,
(2004) 'Mind Over Matter? Collapsing the Mind-Matter Dichotomy in Material Culture Studies', in E. DeMarrais, C. Gosden and C. Renfrew (eds), *Rethinking Materiality: the Engagement of Mind with the Material World*, McDonald Institute Monographs, Cambridge: McDonald Institute for Archaeological Research, 63-71.

BOURRIAU, J. D., NICHOLSON, P. T. & ROSE, P. J.,
(2000) 'Pottery', in P.T. Nicholson and I. Shaw (eds), *Ancient Egyptian Materials and Technology*, Cambridge: Cambridge University Press, 121-147.

BROVARSKI, E.,
(2005) 'Recurrent Themes in the Art of the Predynastic Period', in K. Daoud, S. Beider and A. S. El-Fatah (eds), *Studies in Honor of Ali Radwan*, Cairo: Supplement aux Annales du Service des Antiques de l'Egypte Cahier, 34, 213-240.

BROWN, J. A.,
(1981) 'In Search of Rank in Prehistoric Burials', in R. Chapman, I. Kinnes and K. Randsborg (eds), *The Archaeology of Death*, Cambridge: Cambridge University Press, 25-38.

BRUCK, J.,
(2004) 'Material Metamorphosis: the Relational Construction of Identity in Early Bronze Age Burials in Ireland and Britain', *Journal of Social Archaeology*, 4, 307-333.
(2006) 'Death, Exchange and Reproduction in the British Bronze Age', *European Journal of Archaeology*, 9, 73–101.

BRUNTON, G.,
(1937) *Mostagedda and the Tasian Culture*, London: B. Quaritch LTD.
(1948) *Matmar*, London: B. Quaritch LTD.

BRUNTON, G. & CATON-THOMPSON, G.,
(1928) *The Badarian Civilisation and Predynastic Remains near Badari*, London: B. Quaritch LTD.

CAPART, J.,
(1905) *Primitive Art in Egypt*, translated by A.S. Griffith, H. Grevel: London.

CAPLE, C.,
(2006) *Objects: Reluctant Witnesses to the Past*, New York: Routledge.

CASTILLOS, J. J.,
(1981) 'An Analysis of the Tombs in the Predynastic Cemeteries at Naqada', *JSSEA*, 10, 21-38.

(1982) *A Reappraisal of the Published Evidence on Egyptian Predynastic and Early Dynastic Cemeteries*, Toronto: Benben Publications.

CHAPMAN, J. et. al. (eds),

(1981) *The Archaeology of Death*, Cambridge: Cambridge University Press.

CHAPMAN, J. & GAYDARSKA, B.,

(2007) *Parts and Wholes: Fragmentation in Prehistoric Context*, Oxford: Oxbow Books.

(2009) 'The Fragmentation Premise in Archaeology: From the Palaeolithic to More Recent Times', in W. Tronzo (ed), *The Fragment: An Incomplete History*, Los Angeles: Getty Research Institute, 131-153.

CHILDE, G.,

(1956) *Piecing Together the Past: The Interpretation of Archaeological Data*, London: Routledge.

CONKEY, M. W.,

(1987) 'New Approaches in the search for Meaning? A Review of Research in 'Palaeolithic Art'', *Journal of Field Archaeology*, 14, 413-430.

COSTIN, C. L.,

(1996) 'Exploring the Relationship between Gender and Craft in Complex Societies: Methodological and Theoretical Issues of Gender Attribution', in R.P. Wright (ed), *Gender and Archaeology: Essays in Research and Practice*, Philadelphia: University of Pennsylvania Press, 111-142.

CROSSLAND, Z.,

(2010) 'Materiality and Embodiment', in D. Hicks and M.C. Beaudry (eds), *The Oxford Handbook of Material Culture Studies*, Oxford: Oxford University Press, 333-351.

CRUBEZY, E. et. al.,

(2002) *Adaima 2 - La Necropole Prédynastique*, Cairo: Institut Francais d'Archaeologie Orientale.

DAVID, R.,

(2002) *Religion and Magic in Ancient Egypt*, London: Penguin Books.

DE MORGAN, H.,

(1912) 'Report on Excavations Made in Upper Egypt During the Winter 1907-1908', *Annales du Service des Antiques de l'Égypte*, 12, 20-55.

DI PEDRO, G. A.,

(2011) 'Miscellaneous Artefacts from Zawayda (Petrie's South Town, Naqada), in R. F. Friedman and P.N. Fiske (eds), *Egypt At Its Origins 3: Proceedings of the International Conference 'Origin of the State - Predynastic and Early Dynastic Egypt', London, 27th July - 1st August 2008*, Leuven: OLA 205, 59-79.

DREYER, G. et. al.,

(1998) *Umm El-Qaab, Nachuntersuchungen Im Fruhzeitlichen Konigsfriedhof*, MDAIK, 56, 43-129.

EYCKERMAN, M. & HENDRICKX, S.,

(2011a) 'Tusks and Tags: Between the Hippopotamus and the Naqada Plant', in R.F. Friedman and P.N. Fiske (eds), *Egypt At Its Origins 3: Proceedings of the International Conference 'Origin of the State - Predynastic and Early Dynastic Egypt', London, 27th July - 1st August 2008*, Leuven: OLA 205, 497-570.

(2011b) 'The Naqada I Tombs H17 and H41 at El-Mahasna: A Visual Reconstruction' in R. F. Friedman and P.N. Fiske (eds), *Egypt At Its Origins 3: Proceedings of the International Conference 'Origin of the State - Predynastic and Early Dynastic Egypt', London, 27th July - 1st August 2008*, Leuven: OLA 205, 379-429.

(2012) 'Visual Representation and State Development in Egypt', *Archeo-Nil*, 22, 23-72.

FRIEDMAN, R.,

(2003) 'A Basket of Delights: The 2003 Excavations at HK43', *Nekhen News*, 15, 18-19.

(2008a) 'The Cemeteries of Hierakonpolis', *Archéo-Nil*, 18, 8-29.

(2008b) 'Excavating Egypt's Early Kings: Recent Discoveries in the Elite Cemetery at Hierakonpolis', in B. Midant-Reynes and Y. Tristant (eds), *Egypt at its Origins 2: Proceedings of the International Conference 'Origin of the State. Predynastic and Early Dynastic Egypt', Toulouse, 5-8th September 2005*, Leuven: Peeters, 1157-1194.

(2011) 'Hierakonpolis', in D. C. Patch (ed), *Dawn of Egyptian Art*, London: The Metropolitan Museum of Art, 82-93.

(2013) 'HK Human Figurines', *Nekhen News*, 25, 7.

GAGE, J.,

(1999) 'What Meaning Had Colour in Early Societies?', *Cambridge Archaeological Journal*, 9, 109-126.

GARFINKEL, Y.,

(2003) *Dancing at the Dawn of Agriculture*, Austin: University of Texas Press.

GIMBUTAS, M.,

(1999) *The Living Goddesses*, Los Angeles: University of California Press.

GRAVES-BROWN, C.,

(2010) *Dancing for Hathor: Women in Ancient Egypt*, New York: Continuum.

GELL, A.,

(1998) *Art and Agency: An Anthropological Theory*, Oxford: Clarendon.

GRINSEL, L.,

(1961) 'The Breaking of Objects as a Funerary Rite', *Folklore*, 72, 475-491.

GOSDEN, C. & MARSHALL, Y.,

(1999) 'The Cultural Biography of Objects', *World Archaeology*, 31, 169-178.

GOSDEN, C.,

(2001) 'Making Sense: Archaeology and Aesthetics', *World Archaeology*, 33, 163-167.

(2004) 'Aesthetics, Intelligence and Emotions: Implications for Archaeology', in E. DeMarrais, C. Gosden and C. Renfrew (eds), *Rethinking Materiality: the Engagement of Mind with the Material World*, McDonald Institute Monographs, Cambridge: McDonald Institute for Archaeological Research, 33-40.

HALLAM, E. & HOCKEY, J.,

(2001) *Death, Memory and Material Culture*, Oxford: Berg.

HALVERSON, J.,

(1992) 'Palaeolithic Art and Cognition', *Journal of Psychology*, 126, 221-237.

HAMILTON, N.,

(1996) 'Can We Interpret Figurines?', *Cambridge Archaeological Journal*, 6, 281-307.

HARRINGTON, N.,

(2004) 'Human Representation in the Predynastic Period: The Locality HK6 Statue in Context', in S. Hendrickx, R. Friedman, K.M. Cialowicz and M. Chlodnicki (eds), *Egypt At Its Origins – Studies in Memory of Barbara Adams: Proceedings of the International Conference 'Origin of the State. Predynastic and Early Dynastic Egypt', Krakow, 28th August – 1st September 2002,* Leuven: Uitgeverij Peeters en Departement Oosterse Studies, 27-43.

(2006) 'MacGregor Man and the Development of Anthropomorphic Figures in the Late Predynastic Period', in K. Kroeper, M. Chlodnicki and M. Kobusiewicz (eds), *Archaeology of Early Northeastern Africa: In Memory of Lech Krzyzaniak*, Studies in African Archaeology 9, Poznan, 659-670.

HARTUNG, U. H.,

(2011) 'Nile Mud and Clay Objects from the Predynastic Cemetery U at Abydos (Umm el-Qa'ab)', in *Conference 'Origin of the State - Predynastic and Early Dynastic Egypt', London, 27th July - 1st August 2008*, Leuven: OLA 205, 467-498.

HASSAN, F. A.,

(1992) 'Primeval Goddess to Divine King: The Mythogenesis of Power in the Early Egyptian State', in R. Friedman and B. Adams (eds), *The Followers of Horus: Studies Dedicated to Michael Allan Hoffmann, 1944-1990*, Oxford: Oxbow, 307-322.

(1998) 'The Earliest Goddess of Egypt: Divine Mothers and Cosmic Bodies', in L. Goodison and C. Morris (eds), *Ancient Goddess: The Myths and the Evidence*, London: British Museum Press, 98-112.

(2004) 'Between Man and Goddess: The Fear of Nothingness & Dismemberment', in S. Hendrickx, R. Friedman, K.M. Cialowicz and M. Chlodnicki (eds), *Egypt At Its Origins – Studies in Memory of Barbara Adams: Proceedings of the International Conference 'Origin of the State. Predynastic and Early Dynastic Egypt', Krakow, 28th August – 1st September 2002,* Leuven: Uitgeverij Peeters en Departement Oosterse Studies, 779-800.

HASSAN, F. A. & SMITH, S. J.,
(2002) 'Soul Birds and Heavenly Cows: Transforming Gender in Predynastic Egypt', in S.M. Nelson and M. Rosen-Ayalon (eds), *In Pursuit of Gender: Worldwide Archaeological Approaches*, Walnut Creek: AltaMira Press, 43-65.

HENDRICKX, S.,
(1996) 'The Relative Chronology of the Naqada Culture: Problems and Possibilities', in J. Spencer (ed), *Aspects of Early Egypt*, London: British Museum Press, 36-69.
(2002) 'Bovines in Egyptian Predynastic and Early Dynastic Iconography', in F. Hassan (ed), *Droughts, Food and Culture: Ecological Change and Food Security in Africa's Later Prehistory*, New York: Kluwer Academic Publishers, 275-320.
(2006) 'Predynastic - Early Dynastic Chronology', in E. Hornung, R. Krauss and D.A. Warburton (eds), *Ancient Egyptian Chronology: Handbook of Oriental Studies*, Vol. 83. Leiden, 487-488.
(2011) 'Sequence Dating and Predynastic Chronology' in E. Teeter (ed), *Before the Pyramids: The Origins of Egyptian Civilization*, Oriental Institute Museum Publications, Chicago: The Oriental Institute of the University of Chicago, 15-16.

HENDRICKX, S. & EYCKERMAN, M.,
(2011a) 'Tusks and Tags: Between the Hippopotamus and the Naqada Plant', in R.F. Friedman and P.N. Fiske (eds), *Egypt At Its Origins 3: Proceedings of the International Conference 'Origin of the State - Predynastic and Early Dynastic Egypt', London, 27th July - 1st August 2008*, Leuven: OLA 205, 497-570.
(2011b) 'The Naqada I Tombs H17 and H41 at El-Mahasna: A Visual Reconstruction' in R. F. Friedman and P.N. Fiske (eds), *Egypt At Its Origins 3: Proceedings of the International Conference 'Origin of the State - Predynastic and Early Dynastic Egypt', London, 27th July - 1st August 2008*, Leuven: OLA 205, 379-429.
(2012) 'Visual Representation and State Development in Egypt', *Archeo-Nil*, 22, 23-72.

HENDRICKX, S. et. al.,
(2009) 'Late Predynastic/Early Rock Art Scenes of Barbary Sheep Hunting in Egypt's Western desert: from capturing wild animals to the women of the 'Acacia House'', in H. Reimer, F. Foster, M. Herb and N. Pollath (eds), *Desert animals in the eastern Sahara: Status, economic significance, and cultural reflection in antiquity – Proceedings of an Interdisciplinary ACACIA Workshop held at the University of Cologne, December 14-15, 2007*, Koln: Henrich Barth Institut, 189-262.

HILL, J. & HERBICH, T.
(2011) 'Life in the Cemetery: Late Predynastic Settlement at el-Amrah' in R. F. Friedman and P.N. Fiske (eds), *Egypt At Its Origins 3: Proceedings of the International Conference 'Origin of the State - Predynastic and Early Dynastic Egypt', London, 27th July - 1st August 2008*, Leuven: OLA 205, 109-136.

HODDER, I.,
(1982) *Symbols in Action*, Cambridge: Cambridge University Press.
(2013) *Entangled: An Archaeology of the Relationships Between Humans and Things*, Malden: Wiley-Blackwell.

HORNBLOWER, G. D.,
(1929) 'Predynastic Figurines of Women and their Successors', *The Journal of Egyptian Archaeology*, 15, 29-47.

HOSKINS, J.,
(1998) *Biographical Objects*, London: Routledge.

JONES A.W. & BOIVIN, N.,
(2010) 'The Malice of Inanimate Objects: Material Agency', in D. Hicks and M.C. Beaudry (eds), *The Oxford Handbook of Material Culture Studies*, Oxford: Oxford University Press, 333-351.

KAISER, W.,
(1956) 'Stand und Probleme der ägyptischen Vorgeschichtsforschung', *Zeitschrift fur Ägyptische Sprache und Alterkunde*, 81, 87-109.
(1957) 'Zur inneren Chronologie der Nagadakultur', *Archaeologia Geographica*, 6, 69-77.

KANTOR, H. J.,
(1944) 'The Final Phase of Predynastic Culture Gerzean or Semainean', *Journal of Near Eastern Studies*, 3, 110-136.
KNAPP, B. A. & MESKELL, L.,
(1997) 'Bodies of Evidence on Prehistoric Cyprus', *Cambridge Archaeological Journal*, 7, 183-205.
KNAPPETT, C.,
(2005) *Thinking Through Material Culture: An Interdisciplinary Perspective*, Philadelphia: University of Pennsylvania Press.
KOPYTOFF, I.,
(1986) 'The Cultural Biography of Things: Commoditization as Process', in A. Appadurai (ed), *The Social Life of Things: Commodities in Cultural Perspective*, Cambridge: Cambridge University Press, 64-94.
KRZYSZKOWSKA, O. & MORKOT, R.,
(2000) 'Ivory and Related Materials', in P.T. Nicholson and I. Shaw (eds), *Ancient Egyptian Materials and Technology*, Cambridge: Cambridge University Press, 320-331.
LESKO, B. S.,
(1999) *The Great Goddess of Egypt*, Norman: University of Oklahoma Press.
LESURE, R. G.,
(2002) 'The Goddess Diffracted: Thinking About the Figurines of Early Villages', *Current Anthropology*, 43, 587-610.
(2011) *Interpreting Ancient Figurines: Context, Comparison, and Prehistoric Art*, Cambridge: Cambridge University Press.
MACIVER, D. R. & MACE, A. C.,
(1902) *El Amrah and Abydos, 1899-1901*, London: Egypt Exploration Fund.
MARANGOU, C.,
(1996) 'Assembling, Displaying, and Dissembling Neolithic and Eneolithic Figurines and Models', *Journal of European Archaeology*, 4, 177-202.
MARSHALL, Y.,
(2013) 'Personhood in Prehistory: A Feminist Archaeology in Ten Persons', in D. Bolger (ed), *A Companion to Gender Prehistory*, Oxford: Wiley-Blackwell, 204-225.
MCDERMOTT, L.,
(1996) 'Self-Representation in Upper Palaeolithic Female Figurines', Current Anthropology, 37, 227-258.
MCNAMARA, L.,
(2014) 'The Ivory Statuette from HK6 Tomb 72', *Nekhen News*, 26, 7-9.
MCNAY, L.,
(1992) *Faucault and Feminism: Power, Gender and the Self*, Oxford: Polity Press.
MIDANT-REYNES, B.,
(2000) *The Prehistory of Egypt: From the First Egyptians to the First Pharaohs*, Oxford: Blackwell Publishing.
MESKELL, L.,
(1995) 'Goddesses, Gimbutas, and 'New Age' Archaeology', *Antiquity*, 69, 74-86.
MORRIS-KAY, G. M..
(2010) 'The Evolution of Human Artistic Creativity', *Journal of Anatomy*, 216, 158-176.
MURRAY, M. A.,
(1956) 'Burial Customs and Beliefs in the Hereafter in Predynastic Egypt', *The Journal of Egyptian Archaeology*, 42, 86-96.
NEEDLER, W.,
(1984) *Predynastic and Archaic Egypt in the Brooklyn Museum*, New York: The Brooklyn Museum.
NORDSTROM, H.,
(1996) 'The Nubian A-Group: Ranking Funerary Remains', *Norwegian Archaeological Review*, 29, 17-39.
NOWAK, E. M.,
(2004) 'Egyptian Predynastic Ivories Decorated with Anthropomorphic Motifs', in S. Hendrickx, R. Friedman, K. M. Cialowicz and M. Chlodnicki (eds), *Egypt and Its Origins – Studies in Memory of Barbara Adams: Proceedings*

of the International Conference 'Origin of the State. Predynastic and Early Dynastic Egypt', Krakow, 28th August – 1st September 2002, Leuven: Uitgeverij Peeters en Departement Oosterse Studies, 891-904.

ORDYNAT, R.,

(2015) 'The Female Form: Examining the Function of Predynastic Female Figurines from the Badarian to the Late Naqada II Periods', in J. Cox, C.R. Hamilton, K.R.L. McLardy, A.J. Pettman and D. Stewart (eds), *Ancient Cultures at Monash University: Proceedings of a Conference Held Between 18-20 October 2013 on Approaches to Studying the Ancient Past,* Oxford: BAR International Series, 47-56.

PADER, E. J.,

(1982) *Symbolism, Social Relations and the Interpretation of Mortuary Remains,* Oxford: B.A.R.

PARKER PEARSON, M.,

(1982) 'Mortuary Practices, Society and Ideology: an Ethnoarchaeological Study', in I. Hodder (ed), *Symbolic and Structural Archaeology,* Cambridge: Cambridge University Press, 99-114.

(2003) *The Archaeology of Death and Burial,* Phoenix Mill: Sutton Publishing.

PATCH, D. C.,

(2011) *Dawn of Egyptian Art,* London: The Metropolitan Museum of Art.

PAYNE, J. C.,

(1993) *Catalogue of the Predynastic Egyptian Collection in the Ashmolean Museum,* Oxford: Oxford University Press.

PAYNTER, R.,

(1989) 'The Archaeology of Equality and Inequality', *Annual Review of Anthropology,* 18, 369-399.

PETRIE, W. M. F.,

(1895) *Naqada and Ballas,* London: B. Quaritch LTD.

(1901) *Dispolis Parva: The Cemeteries of Abadiyeh and Hu 1898-9,* London: B. Quaritch LTD.

(1920) *Prehistoric Egypt: Illustrated by over 1,000 Objects in University College, London,* London: British School of Archaeology in Egypt & B. Quaritch LTD.

PEARSON, M.,

(1998) 'Performance as Valuation: Early Bronze Age Burial as Theatrical Complexity', in D. Bailey (ed), *The Archaeology of Prestige and Wealth,* Oxford: BAR International Series, 32-41.

PODZORSKI, P. V.,

(1993) 'The Correlation of Skeletal Remains and Burial Goods: an Example from Naga-ed-Der N7000', in W.V. Davies and R. Walker (eds), *Biological Anthropology and the Study of Ancient Egypt,* London: British Museum Press, 119-129.

POLLARD, C. J.,

(2001) 'The Aesthetics of Depositional Practice', *World Archaeology,* 33, 315-333.

RELKE, J.,

(2001) *The Predynastic Figurines of Upper Egypt,* PhD Dissertation: University of New England.

RICE, P. C.,

(1981) 'Prehistoric Venuses: Symbols of Motherhood or Womanhood?', *Journal of Anthropological Research,* 37, 404-414.

RICHARDS, J.,

(2005) *Society and Death in Ancient Egypt: Mortuary Landscapes of the Middle Kingdom,* Cambridge: Cambridge University Press.

ROBB, J.,

(2015) 'What Do Things Want? Object Design as a Middle Range Theory of Material Culture', *Archaeological Papers of the American Anthropological Association,* 26, 166-180.

ROBERTS, M. N. et. al.,

(1996) 'Body Memory', in M. N. Roberts and A. F. Roberts (eds), *Memory: Luba Art and the Making of History,* New York: The Museum of African Art, 85-116.

ROWLAND, J.,

(2007) 'Death and the Origins of Egypt: Mortuary Variability as an Indicator of Socio-Political Change During the Late Predynastic to Early Dynastic Period', in J. Goyon and C. Cardin (eds), *Proceedings of the Ninth International Congress of Egyptologists, Grenoble, 6 - 12 September 2004, Orientalia Lovaniensia Analecta 150*, Leuven: Peeters, 1629-1643.

RENFREW, C.,

(2004) 'Towards a Theory of Material Engagement', in E. DeMarrais, C. Gosden and C. Renfrew (eds), *Rethinking Materiality: the Engagement of Mind with the Material World*, McDonald Institute Monographs, Cambridge: McDonald Institute for Archaeological Research, 23-31.

SAVAGE, S. H.,

(1997) 'Descent Group and Economic Strategies in Predynastic Egypt', *Journal of Anthropological Archaeology*, 16, 226-268.

(2000) 'The Status of Women in Predynastic Egypt as Revealed Through Mortuary Analysis' in A. E. Rautman (ed), *Reading the Body: Representations and Remains in Archaeological Record*, Philadelphia: University of Pennsylvania Press, 77-94.

SAXE, A.,

(1970) *Social Dimensions of Mortuary Practices*, Unpublished PhD dissertation, University of Michigan.

SCAMUZZI, E.,

(1965) *Egyptian Art in the Egyptian Museum of Turin*, New York: Harry N. Abrams, INC.

SERPICO, M. & WHITE, R.,

(2000) 'Resins, Amber and Bitumen, in P. T. Nicholson and I. Shaw (eds), *Ancient Egyptian Materials and Technology*, Cambridge: Cambridge University Press, 430-474.

SIMON, K. & MACGAFFEY, W.,

(1995) 'Northern Kongo Ancestor Figures', *African Arts*, 28, 48-53.

SPRADLING HOGLUND, K.,

(1983) *The Raised Arm Figurines of Predynastic Egypt: An Analysis and Interpretation*, Ph.D. Dissertation, Northern Illinois University.

STRATHERN, M.,

(1988) *The Gender of the Gift: Problems with Women and Problems with Society in Melanesia*, Berkley: University of California Press.

STEVENSON, A.,

(2007a) 'The Aesthetics of Predynastic Egyptian Burial: Funerary Performances in the 4th Millennium BC', *Archaeological Review from Cambridge*, 22, 75–91.

(2007b) 'The material significance of Predynastic and Early Dynastic palettes', in R. Mairs, and A. Stevenson, (eds), *Current Research in Egyptology 2005: Proceedings of the Sixth Annual Symposium*, Oxford: Oxbow Books, 148–162.

(2009a) 'Social Relationships in Predynastic Burials', *Journal of Egyptian Archaeology*, 95, 175-192.

(2009b) *The Predynastic Egyptian Cemetery of el-Gerzeh. Social Identities and Mortuary Practices.* Leuven: Peeters Publishers.

(2011) 'Predynastic Material Culture', in E. Teeter (ed), *Before the Pyramids: Essays on Earliest Egypt*, Chicago: Oriental Institute Museum Publications, 65-74.

(2013) 'Predynastic Burial Rituals', in R.J. Danna and K. Exell (eds), *Egypt: Ancient Histories, Modern Archaeologies*, New York: Cambria Press, 9-50.

TAINTER, J. A.,

(1978) 'Mortuary Practices and the Study of Prehistoric Social Systems', in *Advances in Archaeological Method and Theory, Vol. 1*, 1978, 105-140.

TALALAY, L. E.,

(1993) *Deities, Dolls and Devices: Neolithic Figurines from Franchthi Cave, Greece*, Bloomington: Indiana University Press.

(1994) 'A Feminist Boomerang: The Great Goddess of Greek Prehistory', *Gender and History*, 6, 165-183.

THOMAS, J.,

(2000) 'Death, Identity and the Body in Neolithic Britain', *The Journal of the Royal Anthropological Institute*, 6, 653- 668.

(2002) *Understanding the Neolithic*, London: Routledge.

TURNER, V.,

(1982) *From Ritual to Theatre: The Human Seriousness of Play*, New York: Performing Arts Journal.

UCKO, P. J.,

(1962) 'The Interpretation of Prehistoric Anthropomorphic Figurines', *The Journal of the Royal Anthropological Institute of Great Britain and Ireland*, 92, 38-54.

(1965) 'Anthropomorphic Ivory Figurines from Egypt', *Journal of the Royal Anthropological Institute*, 92, 214-38.

(1968) *Anthropomorphic Figurines of Predynastic Egypt and Neolithic Crete with Comparative Material from the Prehistoric Near East and Mainland Greece*, London: Andrew Szmilda.

(1969) 'Ethnography and Archaeological Interpretation of Funerary Remains', *World Archaeology*, 1, 262-280.

UCKO, P. J. & HODGES, H.W.,

(1963) 'Some Pre-dynastic Figurines: Problems of Authenticity', *Journal of the Warburg and Courtland Institutes*, 26, 205–22.

VAN GENNEP, A.,

(1960) *The Rites of Passage*, London: Routledge.

VANSINA, J.,

(1984) *Art History in Africa: An Introduction to Method*, London: Longman.

VOIGT, M. M.,

(1983) 'Other Clay Artefacts', in M. M. Voigt (ed), *Hajji Firuz Tepe, Iran: The Neolithic Settlement*, Philadelphia: The University Museum, University of Pennsylvania, 168-203.

(2000) 'Catal Hoyuk in Context: Ritual in the Early Neolithic Sites in Central and Eastern Turkey', in I. Kujit (ed), *Life in Neolithic Farming Communities: Social Organisation, Identity, and Differentiation*, New York: Plenum, 253-293.

VOLKOVA, Y. S.,

(2012) 'Upper Palaeolithic Portable Art in Light of Ethnographic Studies', *Archaeology, Ethnology and Anthropology of Eurasia*, 40, 31-37.

WENGROW, D.,

(2006) *The Archaeology of Early Egypt. Social Transformations in North-East Africa, 10,000–2,650 BC*, Cambridge: Cambridge University Press.

(2011) 'Rethinking 'Cattle Cults' in Early Egypt: Towards a Prehistoric Perspective of the Narmer Palette', *Cambridge Archaeological Journal*, 11, 91-104.

WENKE, R. J.,

(1991) 'The Evolution of Early Egyptian Civilization: Issues and Evidence', *Journal of World Prehistory*, 5, 279-329.

WILKINSON, K. A. H.,

(1996) *State Formation in Egypt*, Cambridge Monographs in African Archaeology, Oxford: BAR International Series.

(2003) *Genesis of the Pharaohs: Dramatic New Discoveries that Rewrite the Origins of Ancient Egypt*, London: Thames & Hudson.

WOODWARD, A.,

(2002) 'Beads and Beakers: Heirlooms and relics in the British Early Bronze Age', *Antiquity*, 76, 1040-1047.